The Morning Hour

Richard Quinney

Borderland Books

Selected and revised from *Oxherding in Wisconsin* ©2013 and *This World of Dreams* ©2014

Published by Borderland Books, Madison, WI www.borderlandbooks.net

Publisher's Cataloging-In-Publication Data

Quinney, Richard.

  The morning hour / Richard Quinney. — 1st edition.

  pages ; cm

  "Selected and revised from Oxherding in Wisconsin ©2013 and This World of Dreams ©2014." — Title page verso.

  Includes bibliographical references.

  ISBN: 978-0-9965052-1-5

  1. Quinney, Richard. 2. Spiritual life. 3. Reality. 4. Farm life. 5. Meditations. 6. Spiritual journals. I. Selections from (work) Quinney, Richard. Ox herding in Wisconsin. II. Selections from (work) Quinney, Richard. This world of dreams. III. Title.

PS3567.U53 Z46 2016

818/.6   2015909516

Designed by Ken Crocker
Production Management by Della Mancuso
Printed by Worzalla Printing

Printed in the United States of America

The morning, which is the most memorable season of the day, is the awakening hour. Then there is least somnolence in us; and for an hour, at least, some part of us awakes which slumbers all the rest of the day and night.

– Henry David Thoreau, *Walden*

Contents

Preface 9

Part I Ox Herding 11

Part II World of Dreams 75

Afterword 165

List of Sections 167

Bibliography 169

Preface

For years, the morning has been my time for contem- plation and of the writing a few words to the day. I remember when this practice began. It was at the end of the summer, at the beginning of a sabbatical leave from New York University. The need for reflection and writing continued in the subsequent years of employment at other universities. My sense of a calling, formed in my early years, was being fulfilled in the course of the daily practice of writing. The urgency to reflect on my life, to give meaning to my existence in this most mysterious and complex world, persisted. Recording my experiences, placing them in a spiritual and intellectual context, became my work and my joy. I could not live otherwise.

The meditating mind, accompanied by writing, is focused, and the present moment is the time of primary importance. Such meditation, as Thomas Merton observed in *New Seeds of Contemplation,* is the highest expression of our intellectual and spiritual life: "It is spontaneous awe at the sacredness of life, of being." It is when we are most fully awake, fully aware and alive.

For nearly a half century, this morning time has been a meditation on the experiences and events of my daily life: the geographical moves, the personal relationships, the thoughts and dreams, the illnesses and recoveries, the reading of books and listening to music, the research and reflections on the lives of my ancestors — all the

things that seemed important to me.

In recent years, I have been thinking and writing about *enlightenment* (what it is and how we might experience it) and *this world of dreams* (the nature of reality as perceived daily). It has become imperative to me, in my eighty trips around the sun, to devote time to these essential concerns. I hope that these writings will be of help to others, and to all those I think and care about in my hours of solitude.

Part I

Ox Herding

MINDFULNESS IN THE MORNING HOUR I write in the morning hour to be aware of the present moment. The mind of the one who writes is open and receptive, floating above the empty page. And what comes to mind may be a thought about something that happened a long time ago. When I place myself in the aura of either the past or the present, I do so in the awareness that I am here, now, in this present moment.

Words by Buddhist monk Achaan Chah have brought me to attention many times before, and serve as an inspiration and guide each morning.

Try to be mindful and let things take their natural course. Then your mind will become still in any surroundings, like a clear forest pool. All kinds of wonderful rare animals will come to drink at the pool, and you will clearly see the nature of all things. You will see many strange and wonderful things come and go, but you will be still. This is the happiness of the Buddha.

Writing meditatively, mindfully, is my still forest pool. My source of reflection and repose.

TRAVELS AT HOME The physical world in which one travels becomes smaller as the traveler ages. I take inspiration from the eighteenth-century French writer Xavier de Maistre, who told of his walks in his bedroom in *A Journey Around My Room.* Later he would tell of going to the window to look into the night sky, in *A Nocturnal Expedition Around My Room.* He was making discoveries in his daily life that had escaped him in former travels. In the foreword to a recent translation of de Maistre's work, Alain de Botton made this elegant observation about de Maistre's journeys at home: "De Maistre's work springs from a profound and suggestive insight: that the pleasure we derive from journeys is perhaps dependent more on the mindset with which we travel than on the destination we travel to. If only we could apply a travelling mindset to our own locales, we might find these places becoming no less interesting than the high mountain passes and jungles of South America." A new-found awareness of the sights, sounds, and daily activities may come when the physical distance that one travels is diminished. In loss there can be something gained.

EVENING PRAYER Lately I have thought about the evening prayer that I would recite each night as a child when my mother put me to bed. Over the years I have wondered whether the prospect of death was a proper subject for a child as the lights were turned off and he was left alone. But I am beginning to realize that the content of that prayer, a Puritan prayer recorded in *The New England Primer,* has provided a spiritual center for my

life. And, at this time in my life, the prayer is becoming
important for the preparations I must make.

Now I lay me down to sleep;
I pray the Lord my soul to keep;
If I should die before I wake,
I pray the Lord my soul to take.

After childhood, I ceased to say an evening prayer.
No petitions were made, no praises were uttered, and
no words of thanks were spoken in prayer. I might have
sensed the need for prayer, but to what or to whom
would I pray? The image of a deity, a god, once available
to the child, had vanished. Other notions of the infinite
and the eternal, however vague, had replaced an image
of a personified deity. And what once was prayer had
become a sustained sense of wonder beyond words.

In years of meditation, I have attended to the unknown and the unfathomable with a quieting of the
mind, contemplation, speculation, and often a letting go
of thought and desire. All the while, I have been thankful for life, and thankful for the real people in my life,
for friends, colleagues, and family. My world — and my
well-being in that world — has been shaped by the attention I have given to my spiritual life. The morning
seasons of the day, the periods of mindfulness, may be
known as prayer.

OX HERDING For a long time writers and artists and students of Buddhism have found spiritual guidance in the parable of the herding of the ox. The material world may be an illusion, with much of human suffering caused by desire and attachment, but understanding and enlightenment are possible in our daily lives.

Ox herding offers instruction on how we might live — not that we will suddenly reach the final stage of enlightenment as a permanent state of being. What we may experience is a momentary revelation in one stage or another, at any given moment. There are days when we may go through several of the stages of ox herding, only to return to the beginning of the search. But the awareness of the possibility of even brief moments of enlightenment is now basic to the living of a life. With attention and practice, ordinary life is a journey toward awareness, understanding, and enlightenment. The ox you are searching for is your own true self.

When you grow up on a dairy farm, as I did, a farm of 160 acres in southern Wisconsin, much of your life is tethered to the barn. The cows in the barn were milked twice each day. At one end of the barn were the stalls filled with calves. At the other end, pacing back and forth in the pen, watching us each morning and night, was the great bull. The chores, their patterns and rhythms, changed with the seasons. The path between the house and the barn was well worn. That path has stayed with me for the whole of my life, no matter how far I traveled from the farm.

The herding of cattle — and the stories of the herding of cattle — began long ago. The cow played an important part in emerging agriculture and was revered as a sacred animal. When attempts were made to give spiritual guidance to daily living, it was to the image of the cow that Hindu storytellers and Buddhist monks turned. Gradually, over a period of at least a thousand years, the parable of ox herding developed, with images and poems and commentaries known today in several versions. The parable is a guide for gaining enlightenment, a way to discover our true nature. The classic story of ox herding tells of ten stages in the course of enlightenment.

ONE Searching for the Ox. The oxherd has lost the ox. He is separated from his true self, the Buddha nature within. He begins searching for what is already there.

TWO Seeing the Tracks. With the help of stories and teachings and sacred texts, the oxherd finds the first traces of the ox.

THREE Seeing the Ox. The oxherd catches a glimpse of the ox. It is only the backside, the heels, and the tail, but it is enough to convince the boy that there is an ox and that he has seen it.

FOUR Catching the Ox. The oxherd finds the ox at the end of the field, and after great effort and struggle, he catches the ox with a rope.

FIVE Taming the Ox. The oxherd keeps a firm hold on the rope as he leads the ox along the path through the pasture.

SIX Riding Home on the Ox. The struggle is over; the oxherd no longer fears losing the ox. With ease the boy rides the ox home.

SEVEN The Ox Forgotten, the Self Alone. The ox has disappeared because the enlightened oxherd is home and no longer needs the ox. The oxherd realizes that the ox is within the one who has been searching.

EIGHT The Ox and the Self Forgotten. Vanished are both the ox and the oxherd. Equanimity prevails. Even the search for the sacred has ended.

NINE Returning to the Source. No need to strive. All things change, and nothing remains the same.

TEN Entering the Marketplace with Helping Hands. Life is in the ordinary living of life — with compassion toward all beings.

The seeker must seek; such is the life of the pilgrim. And this is the core of the existential problem. For the seeker cannot know what is being looked for until it is found. The paradox of ox herding is that the ox from the beginning was never missing. The ox was there all the time, within the seeker. The ox and the seeker are one, from beginning to end. As the Zen master Wuxue Zuyuan wrote in the thirteenth century:

> It's you who are the Buddha, but you just won't see —
> Why go riding on an ox to search for an ox?

The ox that is being sought, the ox that is to be tamed, is one's self. And in the end, an end that can be arrived at daily, the seeker returns to the world of everyday life.

LOVE AMONG THE RUINS Is not the past a sort of ruin? Certainly, the past is an eternity, as Henry David Thoreau envisioned it, just as the future is an eternity — a time everlasting outside the concrete reality of the present. Yet, the remembered past is part of our present reality, and the imagined future shapes our living of the present. Both past and future are ruins in that they are without the substantive reality of the present moment.

The past, as it recedes in time and imagination, disintegrates and falls apart. A weathering takes place, a dilapidation and decay of what once was. All traces of the past may vanish. Or if something remains, something physical or remembered, it is a skeleton of its former self, a remnant that retains its hold on the present. A ghost, welcome or unwelcome, to those who are now living.

I have discovered once again, after an absence of some years, the painting by Edward Burne-Jones titled *Love Among the Ruins.* Originally a gouache painted in the early 1870s, it was damaged a few years later in an attempt to photograph it. Burne-Jones immediately made an oil painting of the same subject, which hangs today in the great parlor of a manor house in England.

The painting was inspired by Robert Browning's poem "Love Among the Ruins." In a meditation on the contrast between past and present, the speaker is in a meadow where sheep are grazing among the ruins of a great city. Armies once marched here, battles were fought, and towers stood tall where now there is a single turret. A girl waits, looking at the place where a king once looked over a city. Nothing is left of what was fought for, and there is nothing to show for the blood that was shed. All has returned to the earth. The poet prefers the grass and the love between the two lovers now meeting among the ruins. Browning ends his poem: "With their triumphs and their glories and the rest! Love is best."

The past is a source of the melancholy and beauty that give depth to our lives in the present. The past adds dimension, a necessary depth, to our daily lives. Life — perhaps at its fullest — is love among the ruins.

THE NATURAL WORLD My spiritual path, even during my early childhood years, has been in the natural world. My sense of the divine has always been grounded in nature. And nature — as the basis of a religious faith — is filled with infinite possibilities. The world of nature is more than we can ever humanly fathom.

Being a naturalist requires a faith that is shared by all religions. One assumes — has faith — that the human mind can understand the natural world. The quantum physicist posits that everything is also something else. Energy, according to such thinking, becomes matter and matter becomes energy, or maybe both at the same time, depending upon our ways of observation. Thus, we living beings are matter today, and we return to energy as the matter of the body decays with death. Nothing is lost in the universe. The atoms that were made at the creation of the universe are the same atoms that are in the universe today. But little is known about the great portion of the universe that is beyond observation. There is scientific speculation on the existence of something conceived of as dark matter.

Much of nature is beyond human observation, just as religious faith is beyond what can be known. Nature, if certainty is desired, is not a substitute for religion. Nature has its own mystery and inability to be known. You could find all the religion necessary in your life by walking through woods or looking into the evening sky, or venturing into the marsh below the farm when you were very young. There is a world of religion outside the theism of any theology.

A Zen teacher reminded me that we all inhabit an illusory world. Our minds — as evolved — perceive a reality that is a function of the human brain. Our minds imagine a reality. Metaphorically, our thoughts are like mice inside a grand piano, never able to see a world outside the confines of the piano.

What we know, what we think we know, is within the boundary of the mind. And, equally, what we believe is bounded by our capacity to believe. Science and religion, necessarily, are both matters of faith. Both give us the illusions by which we live our lives. How precious this life — and how in need we are for the compassion that we give ourselves and one another.

THE EARTH WILL REMEMBER US A long time ago, when living in New York, I recited these lines from a poem by Swedish writer Pär Lagerkvist to my eleven-year-old daughter Laura as we held hands crossing the street:

> One day you will be one of those who lived long ago.
> The earth will remember you just as it remembers
>   the grass and the woods,
> the rotting leaves.
> Just as the soil remembers
> and just as the mountains remember the winds.
> Your peace shall be as unending as the sea.

My daughter expressed interest but said with some humor in her voice that she did not find the words very reassuring. Only later, much later, in one's life could these lines of poetry give some comfort.

I have placed three of my nature photographs in a single frame to form a triptych. My inspiration was a painting for an altarpiece by the nineteenth-century artist Caspar David Friedrich. Titled *The Cross in the Mountains,* it was controversial in its time, because of its unusual treatment of a classic religious theme: a landscape of trees against rays of the setting sun in the encroaching night sky, and, in the distance, a crucifix on a mountaintop. Friedrich originally thought that the painting and accompanying frame would serve as an altarpiece at Tetschen Castle, in Bohemia. Today it hangs in a museum in Dresden, the resting place of a work of religious imagery within the secular world of nature. Nature is celebrated in what continues to be called the Tetschen Altarpiece, and the crucifix is an artifact in the landscape. God has all but disappeared in a scene that depicts the wonder of nature. As in Lagerkvist's poem, the Earth will remember us.

A TRAIN IN THE NIGHT I cannot read often enough the description of traveling on the train between Chicago and Saint Paul that F. Scott Fitzgerald gives to Nick Carraway, the narrator of *The Great Gatsby.* Returning home at Christmastime, Nick is about to leave Union

Station on one of the murky yellow cars of the Chicago, Milwaukee & St. Paul Railroad. He will ride through the countryside of my childhood: "When we pulled out into the winter night and the real snow, our snow, began to stretch out beside us and twinkle against the windows, and the dim lights of small Wisconsin stations moved by, a sharp wild brace came suddenly into the air. We drew in deep breaths of it as we walked back from dinner through the cold vestibules, unutterably aware of our identity with this country for one strange hour before we melted indistinguishably into it again."

This could be a train ride that I took at a time not far removed from that of Nick Carraway and the great Jay Gatsby. I am also, similar to Nick and Gatsby, somewhat removed from worldly life east of the Midwest, but aspire to a life beyond the frontier of my ancestors. Our ancestors came from humble farms of England and Ireland to the New World. I, even at this age, am not far from an old place on top of a hill overlooking a pond at the edge of a marsh.

Do you sometimes think of your life as a story? Do you know that you are the narrator of the story? When you tell others, especially when you write about your life, you are telling a story that has a certain unity, design, and rhythm. You find the patterns that have emerged in the course of your life. Maybe you have already thought about a beginning, middle, and a possible ending. In all likelihood, the story of the life you have created in the living — as well as in the telling — gives meaning each day to your life and provides a guide for the days ahead. We all, as storytellers, make a story of our lives: who we are, where we came from, what we value, what we hope we can give to others, and how we might know peace of mind in our daily lives.

And as we tell our stories, we necessarily return to the past. Not really return, of course, but think about the life once lived, about the people we have known, and the lives that have come before us. My philosophy tells me to live in the present moment, the only time we really have, the here and now. Yet, present moments are enhanced by thoughts of the past. The past is part of the present — in mind and in everyday life. The only nostalgia to guard against is the one that prompts a desire to still be living in the past.

Nick Carraway speaks to Jay Gatsby, who is thinking about his lost love, Daisy, as they stand on the lawn in the evening after the big party at Gatsby's mansion: "You can't repeat the past." Gatsby cries out, "Can't repeat the past? Why of course you can!" Gatsby, Fitzgerald tells us, looks around wildly, "as if the past were lurking here in the shadow of his house, just out of reach of his hand." As the novel ends, so does the life of Gatsby. He has been brought down by the dream that the past can be repeated. We in the New World still want to dream that dream. Fitzgerald ends the novel: "So we beat on, boats against the current, borne back ceaselessly into the past." This is the great American story, a cautionary tale.

THE UNBORN On the cusp of seasons, winter fast fading and spring about to arrive. A sure sign: the turkey vultures have returned. They soar and glide and circle high in the sky, cruising for carrion and refuse, tilting gently from side to side. I count thirteen circling over the woods east of the house. They have scented winter's kill, and will devour and cleanse the ruins of winter. I welcome once again the return of the vultures.

In the ancestral and family stories that I tell, accounts that I find meaningful to my life, I need to keep perspective. I need to be well aware of the mind that is creating these stories and not lose my true self in the drama of the storytelling. Stories give temporal meaning to our lives, but we are always more than the stories we tell. We all have a true nature — a truth — that is absolute and beyond the relativity of our conscious lives.

This ultimate reality that encompasses our relative existence is what Zen masters for centuries have called the *unborn*. Our original and everlasting self, our unborn nature. This is the unborn that is known to us in the teachings and the writings of Zen master Bankei of the seventeenth century. Where were you before you were born? The question gives some comfort as the body shows daily signs of aging.

Patience — and happiness — abides as I sit quietly at the table after the night of falling snow. I meditate on the unborn realm of this infinite and pervasive original mind. *Samadhi* is the Sanskrit word for this composure of mind and body. Moments where you sense the greater reality. Where wisdom and compassion can be found, can be known and practiced in daily life.

Be careful of dwelling entirely in the constructed stories of our lives. At the same time that these stories are being imagined and told, be mindful that they can put us in a dream world apart from who we really are. The stories can separate us from the wholeness of our original nature. And be careful of the stories of loss and sorrow that will cause suffering of the mind. A lament for what no longer exists, a sorrow over the passing of others and other times, will certainly bring suffering. Not all suffering can be eliminated, but we can be aware of our suffering. Be mindful that the past, present, and future are of the same moment.

We move many times daily between a dream world, our constructed reality, and a fleeting glimpse of ultimate reality, the unbornness of our existence. This is one of the great wonders of being human. We are here and elsewhere simultaneously, and sometimes we are consciously aware of this, however fleetingly. Maintaining our balance is another creative adjustment to being human.

Some reminders help us — quotations, pictures, and prayers. For me, often, my instruction is from the allegory of the oxherd. I imagine the herding of the ox — the cow — in the pasture at the farm. Midway across the field, I release my hold on the cow I am herding, and we begin to walk together in harmony. No longer is there the separation, the struggle, between herder and cow. We have become one and the same, and are on the way home. I will go on telling stories — and living this human and temporal life — but sometimes with the awareness and perspective of the unborn.

TELLING THE STORY I am your narrator — the teller of the story and the spinner of tales within the story. I am in the time-honored tradition of the first-person narrator. My narration is also of the subjective mode. Adding to all of this, my telling is a stream of consciousness. And necessarily dictated by the form, I am your "unreliable" narrator, trying with great seriousness to tell you what is happening.

There is no pretension of being an omniscient observer. I am the first-person narrator with a lifetime of experiences that influence what I am seeing now and what I am remembering of the past. As soon as I put my pen to paper, I am in the realm of fiction. In this sense, there is no such thing as nonfiction and no observation that can be objective. The narrator who is telling the story is by definition the main character in the story. Being an "unreliable narrator" is among our human qualities as storytellers. Pretending to know all would be an illusion and a deception. Be true to yourself and your listeners in telling what you know.

Think of yourself, as you tell the story, as being like one of the pilgrims in Chaucer's *The Canterbury Tales*. Or Huck in Mark Twain's *Adventures of Huckleberry Finn*. Or the long-time acquaintance of the old soldier in Ford Maddox Ford's *The Good Soldier*. Or one of the family members carrying the mother's body on the wagon in William Faulkner's *As I Lay Dying*. Or one of the townspeople in Fellini's film *Amarcord*. Or one of the observers in Kurosawa's *Rashomon,* which fifty years ago set me on my course of searching for the multiple realities in the world of everyday life. I can see no other way of being in the world and surviving to tell about it.

Writing in a journal is a presentation of the interior life of the writer. An interior monologue, a stream of consciousness, is being recorded. The emotional, intellectual, and spiritual life of the writer is being revealed to the prospective reader of the journal.

Narrators may well be on a path of increasing awareness of themselves and the world around them as they tell their stories. The narrator is becoming mindful, giving attention to the mind that is telling the story. The mind is being watched as the writing, the telling, is taking place. Writing has become a form of meditation. The writer, likely, is becoming a more compassionate person in the course of mindfully telling the story. The examined mind, in the course of storytelling, is part of the process of increasing compassion. This is the Buddhist meditation, and the practice, of the storyteller.

CALL OF THE SIRENS As dawn with her rose-red fingers shone again, the lustrous goddess Circe warmly hailed Odysseus and his shipmates: "Ah my daring, reckless friends! You who have ventured down to the House of Death alive." She offers food and wine and rest for the livelong day. Taking Odysseus aside, she warns him of the island of the Sirens that his ship must pass on the return to Ithaca. The Sirens — the singing creatures of Greek mythology that beckon sailors to their deaths — are to be avoided.

Odysseus's ship approaches the island, and as it is about to pass, the Sirens burst into their high, thrilling song: "Come closer, famous Odysseus — Achaea's pride and glory — moor your ship on our coast so you can hear our song! Never has any sailor passed our shores in his black craft until he has heard the honeyed voices pouring from our lips, and once he hears to his heart's content sails on, a wiser man."

But Odysseus heeds Circe's warning that the singing is a ruse to lure sailors to their deaths. Odysseus tells his men to put wax in their ears so they will not hear the Sirens. He orders his men to bind him to the ship's mast so that he will not go to the Sirens when he hears their song. When the ship has passed the island and the singing of the Sirens is out of range, Odysseus is freed from the mast. Homer gives us Odysseus's own words, for us to read centuries later: "Once we'd left the Sirens fading in our wake, once we could hear their song no more, their urgent call — my steadfast crew was quick to remove the wax I'd used to seal their ears and loosed the bonds that lashed me." Courage, presence of mind, tactics, and the help of the goddess once again saved Odysseus and his crew.

With some imagination, I am being called by the alluring voices of the Sirens. A year ago Laurie Lewis signed for me a copy of her new album, *Blossoms,* during the intermission of her performance at the High Noon Saloon. Playing now is the final song, "Sirens." Laurie sings, "Somewhere out there I hear the Sirens sing, come on, let go, give in." In another verse she makes her choice: "I stop my ears, for I have made my choice. But oh, the song is so tender." Still, at the end of the song, the Sirens continue to beckon: "Come join our song within the deep green blue." This is just one of the songs that beckons me as I pass other islands.

A song that was popular the year I graduated from high school in Delavan was "You Belong to Me." The singer reminds the one he loves that whatever he is seeing, that person is part of the experience. "See the pyramids along the Nile, watch the sunrise from a tropic isle." Several versions reached the charts in the summer of 1952. The recordings I remember well were by Patti Page, Jo Stafford, and Dean Martin. Such songs continue to draw me to places beyond everyday life. Songs of heart and mind that give gravitas to the days as they go by.

THE MARSH When spring comes each year, my thoughts turn to the marsh on the farm. Spring was, as it still is at the marsh, the warmth of new life spreading over the land as the sun reached higher each day into the sky. Red-winged blackbirds, the first of the birds to return, perched on the cattails. The hills sloping to the marsh began to turn green with fresh and tender grass. In the woods the shooting stars raised their heads toward the sun. The mandrake plant spread its leaves over the early-forming fruit. On the hill north of the marsh the soft leaves of the mullein pushed through the earth. Over the far horizon to the south, great blue herons returned to build their nests in the tamarack trees.

As the spring night unfolded, frogs at the edge of the pond began to peep and croak. The shrill sounds of nighthawks fell sharply through the sky. A pair of

red-tailed hawks nested in one of the tall oak trees.
Muskrats, after resting during the long winter, emerged
from their thatched houses at the edge of the marsh.
Shaking water from their furry bodies, they slipped into
the water and swam away into the reeds and cattails.

I grew to love the marsh and all its creatures and living things. In the years of travel that would follow, what
I had learned from the marsh would serve me well. I was
changing then, as I am still changing, and I was awed by
the mystery of the marsh. This is the renewal, and the
growth, that I know when spring comes each year after
the long winter.

SCHOOL DAYS Each spring, as the snow melts and water begins to flow, I think about the daily adventure of
going to Dunham School in the morning and returning
home in the afternoon. My brother, Ralph, and I would
either walk across the field and through the woods or
ride our bicycles on the gravel road to the school. After
the long winter, and with the warming of the days, water flowed beneath the cracking ice and hardened snow,
down hillsides, and along the edges of the road. One day,
I remember well, I sang all the way to school, "Oh, what
a beautiful morning."

Two recesses a day, plus the noon hour, gave us
time for play. On the baseball field well worn from
seventy-five years of play, we would hit the ball and run

the bases until the school bell called us back to our desks. Often we would ride the aging merry-go-round, swinging around and around and rocking back and forth until it nearly fell off its center pole. Other days we would play Andy-over-the-Schoolhouse, one team throwing the ball high over the roof and tagging each other to increase our team size in the course of the game. One warm spring day, with the smell of peanut butter and jam sandwiches still hanging in the noontime air, we built a grass house over a structure of fallen branches. Some older students later boasted about doing unusual things in the darkness of the grass house.

And each spring, the county school superintendent, Ella Jacobson, visited our school and noted our progress. Studying and learning at Dunham School set the course for the rest of my life. Miss Jacobson wrote these encouraging words on my report card: "Every time I visit this school I find you doing good work. Always do your very best in everything you do. This will bring you success, and you will be happy in your work."

In the spring of 1947, when I finished seventh grade, only five students remained at Dunham School. The school had to be closed until there were more students. I completed the eighth grade at Island School in Richmond Township. That year, for the first time in my life, I felt the reality of change. The transfer to Island School marked the beginning of my move away from home.

THE ETERNAL NOW The first sighting of green shoots coming from the wintering bulbs in the now warming ground. No wonder Easter is the designated springtime event. A resurrection for what seemed to be a death. All around, the stirrings of new life, of life restored. What appeared to be gone is here again.

And again I reach out of need to the high shelf for my daughter Laura's book *William Blake on Self and Soul*. On the cover is the photograph of the life mask of Blake, eyes closed to protect the subject from the drying plaster. Inwardness personified, and I am prompted to explore this self of mine, this self that is connected to everything that exists.

Blake's essential concern is the loneliness of the self, of the soul, because of the subjectivity of the individual. In all of his prophetic writings and drawings, he sought to repair the deep ontological wound. The emotion of "homesickness," the feeling of wandering adrift, is a separation from the transcendent. Such is our existential alienation in the world of everyday life.

Blake gives little thought to an afterlife. The soul is already divine, here and now. This is a new way of living our lives, where the transcendent is imminent. The achievement of the mature soul is to realize that we live in the Eternal Now. We do not wait for a reunion with the divine, with the infinite and the absolute; the union already exists in our lives every day. Our recognition of the transcendent soul gives us access not to the promise of immortality but to the Eternal Now.

At the end of his long prophetic poem *Jerusalem,* Blake begins not with self-transformation, but with love. The inner self turns toward the other. This becomes the true divinity, the capacity of self-sacrifice. These words in the poem capture the significance of our union with others, with the "sacrifice" that is made: "Every kindness to another is a little Death." This is a redefinition of the biblical *agape.* Our true humanity comes in self-sacrifice, when love comes first.

We hope to realize this love and the soul's transformation to the Eternal. My daughter ends her book by reflecting on Blake's final, skeptical thought, with this startling line: "Perhaps the self can neither perfectly right itself nor set itself free from the essential claustrophobia of subjectivity." Maybe this is what it means to be human.

JOURNEY TO A FAR PLACE The theme of journey runs through most memoirs. The life of the author is imagined as being a journey marked by a progression of events and personal awakenings over the course of time. It is not the distance traveled in miles that matters. Physical distance in travel is a metaphor for the course of a life. The metaphor of journey places the life in perspective and gives it coherence. Years ago I described my early life as "a journey to a far place." The "far place," ironically, was the home where I started, a very near place. I had traveled to a place, in my mind, where I could reflect on where I came from and where I was going. Life was consciously being lived as a journey.

I have recently found the poem "Ithaka," by the Greek poet C. P. Cavafy. He was born in Alexandria, Egypt, where his Greek parents had settled. After living in England and working in the family business, he returned to Alexandria and worked for thirty years as a clerk and assistant director in the Ministry of Public Works. In one of Cavafy's most acclaimed poems, he gives us the essence of Homer's *Odyssey*. Our hero, Odysseus, is instructed by the poet:

> Keep Ithaka always in your mind.
> Arriving there is what you're destined for.
> But don't hurry the journey at all.
> Better if it lasts for years,
> so you're old by the time you reach the island,
> wealthy with all you've gained on the way,
> not expecting Ithaka to make you rich.

Yes, the journey itself is the objective, the journey taking precedence over the destination. This is a blessing: a journey lasting for a long time. A journey from your home, from where you began, has served you well.

Served you well because it was origin and destination all in one.

ALL IS DIVINE HARMONY Each time I explore the life of John Muir I find myself in a different place. A new documentary about his life has been presented on the *American Masters* series, titled "John Muir in the New World." I watched the portrayal earlier this week, and for the rest of the week I have been pulling from the shelves John Muir books, and thinking about his life and his mission. That he grew up on a farm in Wisconsin, after emigrating from Scotland with his parents in 1849, during the same migration of my ancestors, adds to my identification with him.

Muir remained deeply religious throughout his life, moving from the Christian theology of supernatural deity to a religion grounded in nature. In the tradition of the transcendentalists, Muir respected and revered nature and found human salvation and redemption in oneness with nature and in protection of the natural world.

As a young man, Muir walked a thousand miles on a journey that took him to the Gulf of Mexico. At the end of the walk he contracted malaria. He booked passage to New York and sailed to California in 1868, where his immense life was lived until his death in 1914. His legacy is assessed at the end of the recent biography by Donald

Worster: "Muir was a man who tried to find the essential goodness of the world, an optimist about people and nature, an eloquent prophet of a new world that looked to nature for its standard and inspiration. Looking back at the trail he blazed, we must wonder how far we have yet to go."

There is an often-reprinted sketch made by Muir on his thousand-mile walk to the gulf. He is sleeping on a grave in Bonaventure Cemetery, three miles from Savannah, near a tributary of the Wilmington River. The following morning he wrote in his journal about the fear of death. He commented on the morbid "death orthodoxy" of civilized Christian religion, observing the rituals and ceremonies that are "haunted by imaginary glooms and ghosts of every degree." What the night in the cemetery, sleeping on the grave, revealed to him, in contrast, was that death is an integral part of nature, part of the renewing cycle of nature. He wrote this about his new understanding of death: "Let children walk with Nature, let them see the beautiful blendings and communions of death and life, their joyous inseparable unity, as taught in woods and meadows, plains and mountains and streams of our blessed star, and they will learn that death is sting-less indeed, and as beautiful as life, and that the grave has no victory, for it never fights." And he added a line now famous and much quoted: "All is divine harmony."

A SHOOTING STAR This day is the day of my mother's birthday. Think of the celebrations and the many anticipations of each birthday. My mother would tell of parties when she was a child with friends and family on the front lawn of her home. My mother nearly reached the birthday of her ninety-third year, short by two weeks at the end of April.

I still watch each spring for the first stems of the shooting star. When young, at the time of my mother's birthday, I would gather bouquets of shooting stars at the edge of the woods and take them to her as my offering of love and a celebration of the arrival of spring.

I have placed again on the table beside my bed the tattered leather-covered Bible inscribed to my mother when she was eleven years old: "Alice M. Holloway, 1917, from Mother and Father." There is a cloth bookmark at the beginning of Ecclesiastes. First verse: "The words of the Preacher, the son of David, king of Jerusalem. Vanity of vanities, saith the Preacher, vanity of vanities; all is vanity." What comes from all our labors under the sun? The fourth verse is of some consolation: "One generation passeth away, and another generation cometh: but the earth abideth for ever."

As a child, my mother had taken care to note John 3:16 on the flyleaf of her Bible and had marked the verse—"For God so loved the world." With the assurance of not perishing, of everlasting life. The Bible is filled between the pages with clippings saved from print-ed matter. One is of "beatitudes for friends of the aged." My mother knew, found comfort in, and gave thanks, sitting at night in the farmhouse: "Blessed are they who make it known that I'm loved, respected and not alone." She was waiting for us to come to her that April morning shortly before another celebration of her birthday.

OUR ANCESTORS What is the first thing that you remem-ber in your life? This will be the event that marks you as a conscious human being and the event that impressed you enough to be committed to memory all these years of your life. This is the event that likely gives you your identity, the primal event that has lasted a lifetime.

For me, it is standing east of the barn, with my father and brother, and watching an old man slowly making his way across the field from the old place. My father tells me that the man is his father. I have no memory of my grandfather before my father said to me that his father was coming across the field to see us. Startled into con-sciousness, I would remember this forever.

I was then nearing the age of five, and my grandfa-ther was in his seventy-eighth year. I am now past his age as he approached for perhaps his last visit to the farm. I do not remember his arrival that day, nor do I remember ever seeing him again. The crossing with recognition of him by my father was everything to me.

My world was the few miles that radiated from the farm to the boundaries of Walworth County. My relatives all lived within a few miles of the farm. The generations before them had settled in the county, and that is where they had lived their lives. Ancestors rest now in the well-kept cemeteries throughout the county. Each Memorial Day, Ralph and I place flowers at the grave sites. Most of all, we remember and celebrate our ancestors, and give thanks for the lives that came before us, giving us our lives.

A METTA BLESSING The Pali word *metta,* known in Buddhist practice as "lovingkindness," embraces the connection of all beings. The practice invites calmness and clarity of mind and heart, and fosters a life of compassion. This is the practice that prepares us for the times ahead — especially the sufferings that come with aging and death. But most of all, this is the practice that is integral to a life well lived. A friend sent me a metta blessing as a birthday wish.

> May you be safe and protected.
> May you be healthy in mind, body and spirit.
> May you be at peace and at ease.
> May you be happy.

My birthday this year ends with a reading of *The Diamond Sutra.* I find solace and relief in a reminder of the impermanence of all things. So much of our suffering comes from the attempt to live with ignorance of impermanence. We spend a lifetime creating things —physical and otherwise — that ultimately must pass away. And, being human, we easily lament the passing and suffer the loss of what we have known in our conditioned existence. At the end of the sutra, variously translated from the Sanskrit, the Buddha responds to questions on the nature of the world as humanly perceived. He says that this conditional existence of ours is like "a flickering lamp, an illusion, a phantom, or a dream." And yet we continue to construct illusions that will explain our experiences and give us comfort in their consequences. This is the source of much of our suffering, when we seek permanence in all things that are transitory, when we try to find answers in a world of illusion.

On good therapeutic and spiritual advice, I am reading and following the meditation practices in Sharon Salzberg's *Lovingkindness: The Revolutionary Art of Happiness*. I would have my religion be kindness, a religion that fosters calmness, clarity of mind and heart, and compassion and understanding. Love, removing us from fear, is the healing force. "When we feel love," says Salzberg, "our mind is expansive and open enough to include the entirety of life in full awareness, both its pleasures and its pains." A loving heart "even for the duration of a snap of a finger, makes one a truly spiritual being." A daily spiritual life is rapture in itself, the kingdom come.

TONGLEN PRACTICE For a long time I have had on my bookshelf, within easy reach, *The Tibetan Book of Living and Dying,* by Sogyal Rinpoche. It presents and clarifies the classic *Tibetan Book of the Dead* and offers meditation practices for Tibetan Buddhism. Twenty years ago, when Sogyal Rinpoche's book was published, I read portions and wrote at the front that I will return to this book in time of need. The *Tonglen* practice of Tibetan Buddhism is informing my thought and spiritual life.

Tonglen in Tibetan is "giving and receiving." It is a practice of opening yourself to the truth of suffering, to the suffering of the self and the suffering of others. Rinpoche writes: "No other practice I know is as effective in destroying the self-grasping, self-cherishing, self-absorption of the ego, which is the root of our suffering and the root of all hard-heartedness."

Evoking compassion is the beginning of the practice. A range of methods is given, starting with a meditation on lovingkindness. "Let your heart open now, and let love flow from it: then extend this love to all beings." Throughout the practice, the movement is toward a compassionate wish to attain enlightenment for the benefit of others. "In the Tonglen practice of giving and receiving, we *take* on, *through compassion,* all the various mental and physical sufferings of all beings: their fear, frustration, pain, anger, guilt, bitterness, doubt, and rage, and we *give* them, *through love,* all our happiness,

and well-being, peace of mind, healing, and fulfillment."
As I breathe in, I am taking in the suffering of all beings,
my own included, and as I breathe out, I am giving love
and happiness and wishes of well-being.

The practice of Tonglen is known by many names in
all religious and spiritual traditions. A better world, here
on Earth, will come with the everyday, noble practice
of giving unto others, giving unto others as you would
compassionately give unto yourself.

AND THEN WHAT? I have received from the biographer
of Glenway Wescott a manuscript of the last journals
written by Wescott. After many years of researching, collecting, and editing the journals, Jerry Rosco provides
the last entry made by Wescott three years before dying
in 1987. It was Memorial Day, and he wrote: "Is it possible that I may fail to ever write again? Again and again
in the early morning I take a page of the pink paper that
delights me, punched three times for my habitual three-
ring binders, and then what?" Wescott valued the craft
of writing to the end. Writing daily in the journal was
among the last things to go.

Much earlier in his life, when he was in his twen-
ties, Wescott traveled by train from Chicago to the small
town in central Wisconsin where his parents were living after retiring from farming at the edge of the Kettle
Moraine. He had already been to Europe, living among

the expatriate writers, and he was returning for a visit during the Christmas holiday. Wescott described the journey on the train, his days of visiting, and his reflections on Wisconsin and the Midwest in the introduction to the book he published in 1928 as *Goodbye, Wisconsin*.

This from Wescott's writing on leaving Wisconsin on the train in the night: "Over many little bridges the train makes a soft thunder. A piece of moon has come up. In front of it a grove of naked trees, a flat expanse of dreary silver tarnished by weed-tops thrusting through it, a broken-looking house, a town, a living but icy river, rapidly give place to each other; as in the foreground of a writer's attention possible subjects for a book vary and shift before that waxing, waning, one-sided radiance which is his own spirit and about which alone he has no choice." Wescott, from a farm in Wisconsin, lived the writer's life for the rest of his life.

I write this now in my treasured three-ring binder. Below my window, this day in early June, the peonies are blooming gloriously all over the lawn. The shades of red and pink. And then what?

THE PASTURE AT THE FARM Hot and humid air expands north from the south as high pressure builds at all levels of the atmosphere. A combination of heat, humidity, and sunshine will create dangerous conditions. Temperatures today will climb toward a hundred degrees, and we are warned that humidity will become oppressive. The weather brings us to attention.

And how is the farm boy as he herds the cows in the pasture east of the barn? We keep an eye on him as he rounds up the cows for another evening of chores. He came to mind again last night as I continued my reading of *Falling into Grace* by Adyashanti. The author reminds us, as he recounts his own spiritual development, that "awakening," or "enlightenment," is not a goal to be reached one time only. There is no end point in a spiritual life, but we are always in the process of awakening into another reality. Spiritual awakening comes with the letting go of the self-centeredness of striving for enlightenment. By letting go of the suffering caused by the desire to be enlightened. He writes, "People in the spiritual world are often busy meditating, chanting the name of God, and doing various spiritual practices and prayers as a means of trying to bring happiness to themselves or to garner God's grace. Spiritual people often listen to the teachings of great awakened ones and try to apply them, but they often miss the key element, and that is: We're addicted to being ourselves. We're addicted to our own self-centeredness. We're addicted to our suffering. We're addicted to our beliefs and our worldview. We really think that the universe would collapse if we relinquished our part in it. In this way, we actually want to continue suffering."

Herding the ox, no matter how the stages are conceived and divided, is movement out of the dream world of the mind and into the world of reality. Adyashanti reminds us that awakening comes in the recognition of the unborn. "The invitation is for all of us to stay in beginner's mind, to always stay in touch with the unborn, the undying, and the uncreated, because it's from that potential that something in us awakens that is free from strife and suffering and that has been waiting in every single one of us to express itself." Our lives become "an expression of that which is inexpressible, unexplainable, and indefinable." All is possible in the pasture at the farm.

THE DIARY OF 1939 When clearing out the farmhouse, I found in the desk drawer the diary that Mabel Stiles Holloway kept for the year 1939. Mabel married my grandfather Will Holloway in 1924, several years after the death of my grandmother Lorena, my mother's mother. We often visited my grandfather and Mabel, and they came to visit us several times each week. Our family would drive the three miles north to Millard to spend evenings, often joined by Mabel's two sisters and their families. Evenings usually ended with the serving of a cake or pie baked that day by Mabel.

As I read Mabel's diary of 1939, the year that I was five years old, I am placed in a world that I was just beginning to know. And slowly reading the diary, I find myself entering the lives of those now gone. And, in a mysterious way, I have a sense that I am continuing to live their lives. Living their lives as might be understood through quantum physics or spiritual mysticism, or through the biological memory of DNA, or through the good example of how they lived. Our ancestors are with us always.

I am impressed with the great amount of activity that filled the days of my grandfather and Mabel. There were daily trips to towns nearby — Delavan, Elkhorn, Fort Atkinson, Whitewater — and to towns and cities farther away at least once a week — Madison, Janesville, Racine. As clerk of Sugar Creek Township, my grandfather often had business to attend to, taking him and Mabel to various meetings and public events. They visited, or were visited by, relatives almost daily. And there were the trips to doctors and dentists and the shopping trips for food, clothing, and hardware.

This was a community. At random, an entry for November 7: "Tuesday evening. We went to a 4-H banquet at Tibbets. Johnsons and Fosses were there, too. Will was called on to make a few remarks." The next day, November 8: "I helped at Methodist Church in Delavan. They served chicken pie for their annual supper. They had a swell supper. We left about 7:30 p.m. for home and to get ready for another celebration, Paddock's 40th wedding anniversary. Willard and family and Dewey and Lizzie called for us — we took a cake (Sunshine) — each family gave a quarter. They served a nice lunch and had a fine program. I had rather a full day. Furnished one chicken for the Methodist supper."

Recorded is the funeral of my grandfather John Quinney. I note the purchase of "caps for the Quinney boys for their birthdays." Thanksgiving Day is celebrated at the home of Mabel's sister and family — the Millers — in Fort Atkinson. At the end of December, Mabel writes that they have received sixty-five Christmas cards. The journal closes: "Good-by Old Year with all your joys and sorrows! We turn our faces toward the dawn of a new Year."

I visited Mabel for the last time in 1961, at the Homestead Convalescent Hospital in Delavan, where she was spending her final days. I had returned from upstate New York where I was beginning my first year of university teaching. Two years earlier, my grandfather had been struck and killed by a speeding car as he was walking home from the Millard grocery store. Gone, the generation of grandparents. Life would have to be lived in other ways.

CROSSING THE STREET Early in the morning my doctor called to tell me that the surgery scheduled for two weeks from now must be cancelled. Results from a physical examination last week indicate the need for more tests to determine if I have too many risk factors for the surgery.

Appointments are being made with cardiologist, urologist, and neurologist. As my friend Gordon, a doctor, tells me, my case is complex. Again, I am being reminded of the clear and present signs of aging, my aging.

My daughter Laura came for a visit during the weekend. She and I had crossed many streets together before, but this time I was having difficulty walking securely as we were about to cross the street on our way to the car after attending a friend's opening exhibition of photographs. Laura offered me her arm for help — and I had the surprising and spontaneous reaction of wanting to avoid assistance, followed immediately by a mixture of gratitude and acceptance. In the few short steps with my daughter, I was learning something new, and I was becoming aware of the present reality.

I am reading carefully the passages on the management of pain and suffering in Sharon Salzberg's *Lovingkindness*. She writes: "We are brought up with the feeling that suffering is somehow wrong or to be avoided. We get the idea that suffering is unbearable and should not even be faced." Acknowledging our suffering, and opening to it, is relief from a burden. Awareness of the infirmities now experienced in my life is recognition of what is true. And recognizing the truth, beyond illusion, is the first step in developing compassion. Compassion for oneself and compassion for all others.

Without judgment, we see that some things bring pain and some things bring happiness. We can learn to act without the effects of aversion. Salzberg writes, "To view life compassionately, we have to look at what is happening and at the conditions that gave rise to it." This life is an expression of what we understand, care about, and value. May the suffering of aging help me to be more compassionate in my daily life.

THE BLACKSMITH In the box marked "Unknown" I have found a photograph made in the late 1860s or early 1870s that I can now identify as being a portrait of my mother's great-grandparents James and Joyce Wishart. The Wisharts emigrated from England in 1828, settling in Clinton, New York, and moved by boat and wagon to LaGrange, Wisconsin, in 1844. Their youngest child, Ellen, would later marry Charles Taylor, and Charles and Ellen would give birth to Lorena, who would marry Will Holloway and give birth to my mother.

James and Joyce Wishart were accompanied to La-Grange by John Wishart, the Scottish father of James, and his Scottish wife, Ann Stockdale. Descendants to this day note the martyrdom of George Wishart, who was burned at the stake by the Catholic Church for heresy in Saint Andrews, Scotland, in 1546, and honorably claim him as an ancestor.

James had apprenticed to the trade of blacksmithing before emigrating. He continued to be a blacksmith in LaGrange, as well as a farmer, until he died in 1882. Joyce died two years earlier. They were the parents of eight surviving children. In the portrait of James and Joyce near the end of their pioneering lives, James holds a family Bible.

Among my mother's books was a signed copy of *The Blacksmith's Daughter,* by Cecile Houghton Stury, granddaughter of James and Joyce. Much can be learned about the lives of the LaGrange pioneers from the stories that James and Joyce's daughter Elizabeth passed on to her daughter Cecile. I pay particular attention to the fact that some of the blacksmithing of James was the shoeing of oxen. The oxen pulled wagons and plowed the fields—"gee" for a right turn and "haw" for a left turn. An ox could get through the deep snow better than a horse could. A team of oxen was highly valued on the prairie at the edge of the Kettle Moraine. I imagine James in his blacksmith shop sharpening plow points, with sparks flying from the anvil as the hammer struck, and nailing the shoes to the hooves of the oxen. "Father keeps all the records in a big book of what men owe him and when he collects all of it we will have our home paid for. Nobody can make us move." I have heard from a descendant that the ledger has been found in a trunk stored in a farm shed of a child of James and Joyce who moved from LaGrange when young to homestead in Mapleton, Minnesota.

We realize, finally, in the allegory of ox herding, that the ox was never lost. How could the ox be lost when our true nature was there from the beginning? All things are an intimate part of the entire cosmos. Nothing needs to be sought; nothing needs to be gained. The treasure is already here, within us and related to everything else, and is always changing.

EQUANIMITY Aversion to aging and physical deterioration is a hindrance, in the Buddhist sense, to the lessening of suffering. Readily coming to mind throughout the day, as I take another painful step and as I receive another call from the clinic or the hospital for another medical test, is the thought that this should not be happening to me and that once I was not in this condition, that things should be otherwise. I spend energies trying to push away — to avert — what is really happening. But this I also know: pain and suffering can be alleviated when I can see things as they are, when I recognize impermanence and the changing nature of everything, when I see the constant flow of events that are outside my control, when I cease to make judgments about the way things are. In other words, when I relax to the wise and compassionate state of being that is known as *equanimity*.

Equanimity, imagined visually, is when the ox-herd in the allegory achieves harmony with the ox that is being herded. Imagine the boy in the pasture at the farm walking home in harmony with the cow. Life is in balance.

With the gift of equanimity, as Salzberg notes in her book, suffering can be accepted without aversion:

"Thanks to the gift of equanimity, we can develop the courage to stay open to suffering. We can face pain again and again without being overcome by sorrow and misery, without becoming so embittered by them that we have to strike out at them and push them away." In the daily practice of equanimity, one can be at home with things as they are.

And yet, on some days, and often on the same day that I am in harmony with the ox, I am also in agreement with Dylan Thomas's cry into the abyss:

Do not go gentle into that good night,
Old age should burn and rave at close of day;
Rage, rage against the dying of the light.

This, as well, is the way things really are. Such is the complex nature of being human and mortal.

A GREAT ADVENTURE Sometimes, still, I wake up in the morning from dreaming that I am young and ready to begin a great adventure. Sometimes I am contemplating what direction my life could take, what my occupation in life might be. I still have a sense that I am waiting to be called.

One of my earliest inspirations came from reading the autobiography of the explorer and paleontologist Roy Chapman Andrews. I was a freshman in high school in Delavan, in 1948, and I had been browsing in Abrams Public Library in town, before driving home for evening chores. I took from the shelf the book with the brown and yellow jacket that pictured a camel caravan crossing the Gobi Desert. The book was titled *Under a Lucky Star.* I learned immediately that the author was born and grew up just a few miles away, in Beloit. If a boy from Wisconsin, from my part of Wisconsin, could become an explorer and discoverer of dinosaur eggs in the Gobi Desert, what might be possible for me?

After a childhood of exploring the natural world along the Rock River and in the woods and fields of southern Wisconsin, Andrews attended Beloit College. After graduation he traveled to New York and asked for a job at the American Museum of Natural History, where he started as a sweeper of floors and eventually became a naturalist, explorer, and director of the museum. Andrews led a series of daring journeys, known as the Central Asiatic Expeditions, into uncharted expanses of Mongolia, and unearthed a treasure-trove of fossils of dinosaurs and many species of extinct reptiles and mammals. The expeditions constituted one of the most innovative episodes in the annals of scientific discovery. The autobiography, which includes accounts of these expeditions, is today regarded as one of the best science books ever written.

In memory of Roy Chapman Andrews, and in recognition of the importance of the book in my own life,

I republished *Under a Lucky Star*. I made certain that Chapman's reflection about his own calling would be printed on the jacket of the book: "From the time that I can remember anything I always intended to be an explorer, to work in a natural history museum, and to live out of doors. Actually, I never had any choice of profession. I wanted to be an explorer and naturalist so passionately that anything else as a life work just never entered my mind." Andrews maintained a sense of wonderment throughout his life. He has been an inspiration to me throughout my life, and continues to be a source for embracing the adventures of life.

ONCE UPON AN ISLAND Once upon a time, on the island of Manhattan, I walked its streets and byways, camera in hand, seeing things I had never seen before. I eventually published a book of photographs from that time and place in my life. At the beginning of the book, I used as an epigraph lines from Walt Whitman's *Leaves of Grass:*

> The question, O me! so sad, recurring — What good
> amid these, O me, O life?
>
> *Answer.*
> That you are here — that life exists and identity,
> That the powerful play goes on, and you may
> contribute a verse.

For over thirty years I kept the photographs I had taken on the island as the decade of the sixties was ending. As I moved from one place to another, the sleeves of negatives and the trays of slides moved with me. Someday, I thought, the documentation might serve some unforeseen purpose. If nothing else, the photographs would show the passing of time and the changing of the landscape. I did not know, until September 11, 2001, that the photographs would take on a meaning and significance beyond anything I could have imagined. Always, as with all photographs, we know that their use and meaning will eventually go beyond anything we can now imagine. Photographs are a reminder of the impermanence of all things.

Living in New York, I thought then that I was at the center of the world. I was part of the movements of the 1960s — civil rights, antiwar protest, counter-culture, the war on poverty, avant-garde theater, and pop and radical art. Construction of the World Trade Center was taking place in the dynamic social and political context of the times. Lyndon Johnson had been elected president in 1964 to deliver the programs of the Great Society and to solve — or at least improve upon — the nation's problems of poverty, inequality, education, and urban decay. Yet the escalation of U.S. military intervention in Southeast Asia — half a million troops in Vietnam by the end of 1967 — caused cutbacks to domestic programs.

Opposition to the war increased, and there were protest marches down Fifth Avenue and bus rides to Washington for huge antiwar demonstrations.

At New York University, where I was teaching, we were questioning not only the war, but also the role of the university. In Washington Square and in the East Village, along First Avenue and Second Avenue and in Tompkins Square Park, another form of resistance was taking place. Hippies and flower children, as the media called them, were on the streets and in the lofts. Abbie Hoffman came to my sociology class, and *Hair* opened at the Public Theater. We were shocked and shaken by the assassinations of Martin Luther King Jr. and Robert Kennedy. Exhausted by the protests against his Vietnam policies, President Johnson announced that he would not run for re-election, and in January of 1969 Richard Nixon was inaugurated as president. In the summer of 1969, police raided the Stonewall Inn on Christopher Street, a riot ensued, and the movement for gay rights began.

I was fascinated that I was living on an island, the island of Manhattan. The waters of the Hudson River, East River, Harlem River, and New York Bay surrounded the island. Walking the edges of the island, the thirty-five miles of shoreline, became a metaphor for the way I was experiencing my own life.

In 1968 I began to photograph in ways I had never photographed before. I was instructed and inspired by the photographers collectively known as the concerned photographers. I took courses with Sandra Weiner and Cornell Capa, and I met other photographers who were exploring the new cultural landscape. For two years, my last two years in New York, I photographed almost daily what I was seeing and experiencing. Usually I used black-and-white film in a 35mm camera. For several months, with color slide film in my camera, I walked to Lower Manhattan and photographed the construction of the World Trade Center. The opposing and conflicting dynamics of the times, as the sixties were ending, could be seen as one world was coming down and another was going up.

As I walked with my camera along the streets of Lower Manhattan, at the construction site, I observed the times in a microcosm. My self-proclaimed project as a sociologist and photographer was to document the changes that were taking place. The public had not generally endorsed the building of the World Trade Center. Many regarded the project as the triumph of corporate business over the public interest. Local merchants were losing their shops and the neighborhood was vanishing, bulldozed to make way for corporate headquarters. The police heavily patrolled the area. Construction workers boldly displayed the American flag, and protesters of the war and the construction were present daily.

There was excitement and fascination with the construction of this major building project by the employees on Wall Street, by nearby residents, by visitors to the city, and by much of the population of Manhattan. The sounds were of jackhammers and pile drivers, the constant grind and roar of heavy equipment, and the voices of the workers. And there were the moments of repose, workers lunching and taking breaks, talking to each other. Men and women stood quietly and viewed the site. Vendors sold their wares from the street. And there was the photographer — inspired — releasing the shutter of the camera with great joy. With hopes of contributing a verse to the great play that was going on.

NOT TO BE FORGOTTEN As the arc of the summer sun begins to lower, we remember the later days of our voyager, Odysseus. He is still wandering, roving through the towns, well-planed oar on his shoulder, with thoughts of the journey home. Knowing the words of the prophet, he speaks of ripe old age and what must be:

> And at last my own death will steal upon me ...
> A gentle, painless death, far from the sea it comes
> To take me down, borne down with the years in ripe
>   old age
> With all my people here in blessed peace around me.
> All this, the prophet said, will come to pass.

His wife, Penelope, hopes for a happy old age.

In the meantime, not to be forgotten, in spite of what will come to pass, or because of what will come to pass, is the understanding of our true home. Astronomically, everything in the universe is moving away from everything else. There is no fixed reference point in the universe that we can call home. Every point, then, is home; we are at home everywhere.

We are an intimate part of everything, of the great evolving whole, rather than separate and isolated individuals without a home. We abide everywhere, aware that our ultimate existence is beyond this body that we know existentially as our own. We are aware of this especially in times of sickness, old age, and death. I read again, as reminder, the paragraph from Salzberg's *Lovingkindness:* "When we identify with the body as a separate self, as our only home, we think we must control it in order to preserve our sense of who we are. But we cannot control sickness or old age or death. If we try, we bear the inevitable burdens of hopelessness and powerlessness. When we conceive ourselves as finite and separate, how fearful death becomes! What would we fear if we experienced ourselves to be part of the whole of nature, moving and changing, being born and dying?"

We — our minds and our bodies — are joined in all of the matter, energy, and spirit of the universe. Each breath we take, each breath we make, is a joining with everything that is beyond the self that we narrowly conceive as distinct and separate, permanent and unchanging.

A morning message from a friend tells me that he had breakfast with a friend and asked him what he means by *spiritual*. His friend, a man of considerable age, answered, "I think of its root: to inspire, as in breathing." Just the breathing, that we are here, that we exist, that we are breathing to keep alive. No other visions, miracles, rituals, or doctrines are needed this day.

IN THIS WORLD Extreme heat continues through the week in the heartland. Temperatures of one hundred–plus degrees are combined with high humidity and sunshine. There are warnings to drink plenty of water, wear light-colored clothing, and avoid strenuous activity.

From across the room, this morning hour, Van Morrison is singing his stream of consciousness song "Madame George." A spiritual sense of desire and loss and remembrance of things past.

> That's when you fall
> When you fall into a trance
> Sitting on a sofa playing games of chance
> With your folded arms in history books you glance
> Into the eyes of Madame George.

Say good-bye to Madame George and dry your eyes for Madame George and wonder why for Madame George. "Get on the train, get on the train."

The Dalai Lama tells an audience in Chicago that everyone wants a happy life. That happiness begins with honesty, which creates trust, which leads to friendship, which means happiness. Religion has nothing to do with it, he tells the audience, adding that moral principles are not rooted in religious doctrine but in the pursuit of happiness.

The morning newspaper reports that the crisis over the extension of debt limits in the United States, debated by Republicans and Democrats, is nearing the default deadline. The spacecraft *Atlantis,* in its last flight, is on its way back to Earth. There is a change of generals in the Afghan War. Severe drought and famine are taking place in Somalia. In this world of our making, what center is there to hold on to? My heavy head spins at once with the universe. The Indian guru in Somerset Maugham's novel *The Razor's Edge* speaks of the infinite goodness of the universe, of which we are inevitably part and parcel.

It is to the book that I again turn for a grounding of mind and body and spirit. This is another way of returning to the herding of the ox, to walking peacefully in happiness with the ox that was thought to be missing. Near the end of Zen master Adyashanti's *Falling into Grace,* I am reminded that it is vitally important that we understand that we regularly inhabit two different worlds.

One world, the one we humans are born into, is the world of opposites, the world of relativity. A world composed of good and bad, of love and hate, of distinctions that make sense for living in the world we humans have created. This is the conventional world we live in most of the time.

But there is another world, a whole other state of consciousness that is beyond the world of duality, beyond the relativity of conventional human existence. This other world is what Jesus referred to as "the kingdom of Heaven." This is what the Buddha called *nirvana* — life lived outside the realm of relativity, outside the ego of conventional consciousness.

We cannot live without being a part of the conventional, dualistic world. We have to function in the relative world in order to survive. But with an awareness of mind we can, as various Buddhist masters have instructed, "abide in non-abiding." We can, following the words of Jesus, be "in this world, but not of it." We can live in both the world of relativity and the world of ultimate reality. Our human existence includes the relative, but it is not entirely defined by relative reality. Adyashanti writes this about the consciousness of living in both worlds simultaneously: "This state of consciousness is the hardest place to describe, because it is literally indescribable. The highest reality is being both 'this' and 'that' and neither; being both spirit and human; being a field of open, spacious awareness, as well as one particular human incarnation. This is something that takes great subtlety, a deep willingness to go beyond all of our notions, even our notions of good and bad, and right and wrong."

A letting go, a surrendering, to the search and quest for spiritual enlightenment. The ox was never missing; the divine is always present. From *Falling into Grace:* "When we look out the window, there's a tree, a garbage can, the grass, a flower, a human being. All of this is actually the face of God. Look in the mirror; that's what God looks like today. Look out the window; that's your true self. That's your true nature being manifest at this moment." No place to go, nothing to run away from, because there is nowhere to go. "Here is the only place there is." My prayer is a letting go, an opening of the self to the whole world.

A POSTCARD You look at the painting by Georges-Pierre Seurat titled *Sunday Afternoon on the Island of La Grande Jatte,* completed in 1886. Your eye optically connects the dots of paint to make new colors. I have done this several times on my visits to the Art Institute of Chicago.

This week I have been watching the film *Sunday in the Park with George* by Stephen Sondheim and James Lapine, the musical that explores the Seurat painting. The figures in the painting come to life, their stories are told, and the life of the painter is examined. A dedicated artist, Seurat did not always connect the dots in his own life; he held relationships at a distance. But on canvas, from the blank canvas, he painted and created images of beauty. I watch and listen again to Sondheim's song "Finishing the Hat." Seurat, played by Mandy Patinkin, stands at the window in Paris, watching the rest of the world, and paints. "Mapping out a sky." "What you feel like, planning a sky." "Studying the hat." "Standing back to look at a face." "There's a part of you always standing by." "Finishing a hat." And the lines of epiphany at the end of the song: "Look, I made a hat... / Where there never was a hat."

My daughter and her family are in Paris. She sends me photos from her cell phone of the places I used to take her when visiting Paris forty-some years ago. I watched, long ago, as she played for whole afternoons in the Luxembourg Gardens. To my grandsons, as they prepared for their first trip to Paris, I sent the words from the ending of Ernest Hemingway's *A Moveable Feast*. Each time that I have gone to Paris I have read these lines and copied them into my travel journal: "There is never any ending to Paris and the memory of each person who has lived in it differs from that of any other. We always returned to it no matter who we were or how it was changed or with what difficulties, or ease, it could be reached. Paris was always worth it and you received return for whatever you brought to it."

I have found in one of my great-aunt Kate's albums a picture postcard sent to her from Paris in the summer of 1906. Kate, my grandfather Quinney's sister, was working in Chicago then as a seamstress and hat maker. She made fine hats for the wealthy society women of Chicago, from materials purchased at Marshall Field. The postcard is from "Inga," one of the women who would be wearing a hat made by Kate. On the front of the postcard, she wrote that Paris is "a very gay place," and that she is having a nice time. Kate never went to Paris. When she retired she returned to the house on the farm at the old place.

PREPARE A SHIP Many times over the course of this year I have thought of D. H. Lawrence. Of his life, his novels, short stories, and travel writings, and his poems. I knew that I must eventually write a few words in my journal about Lawrence. He suffered from tuberculosis much of his life, moved from one residence to another, and died in 1930. His life and work are well documented in John Worthen's *D. H. Lawrence: The Life of an Outsider*. Earlier this year I purchased a used copy of Lawrence's *Last Poems,* published posthumously. His religious poem "The Ship of Death" is important for my journal. The poem, remaining in fragments, was being written as he lay dying.

We know from the introduction to *The Complete Poems* that Lawrence's last poems were influenced by his exploration and study of Etruscan tombs in Italy. Lawrence wrote: "To the Etruscan all was alive; the whole universe lived; and the business of man was himself to live amid it all. He had to draw life into himself, out of the wandering huge vitalities of the world. The cosmos was alive, like a vast creature." The force could be known as God, or as the gods, and as the soul of our being.

Lawrence leads us into the underworld of mythology. He tells us that in the Etruscan tombs he saw "the sacred treasures of the dead, the little bronze ship of death that should bear him over to the other world, the vases of jewels for his arraying, the vases of small dishes, the little bronze statuettes and tools, the armour." From Lawrence's last poem, "The Ship of Death":

> Have you built your ship of death, O have you?
> O build your ship of death, for you will need it.

And at the end of the poem, with wonder and reverence, is a vision of resurrection. "The frail soul" steps out of the ship, heart filled with peace.

SWALLOWTAIL BUTTERFLIES Two large butterflies flutter daily from bush to bush and flower to flower on the lawn. I watch for long periods of time from the balcony of my house. These swallowtails, in all their beauty, are in the summer stage of their cycle of life.

The swallowtail butterfly in its life cycle changes from egg to caterpillar to chrysalis to the adult butterfly that is giving such pleasure these days of summer. In the process called *metamorphosis*, the fully formed swallowtail emerges from the pupal case, finds nourishment in the garden, mates with another swallowtail, and lays eggs in the vegetation. Before summer ends, a caterpillar that emerges from an egg will feed and shed its skin several times as it grows. It will find a safe place for the creation of the wondrous chrysalis, from which one day a swallowtail will emerge, drying its moisture in the sun, and taking flight as life continues into another summertime.

INTER-BEING Many of the ideas and thoughts that first come to us in words — in conversations with others and in our solitary reading — become integral to our lives. A word that I have remembered for years, and have tried to incorporate into my life, is the word *inter-being,* which Vietnamese Buddhist master Thich Nhat Hanh uses in his writings and teaching. Nothing exists by itself alone; everything depends on every other thing. From this perspective, all being is inter-being.

Always absent in all that exists is a separate self, and in Buddhism this is called *emptiness.* An example of impermanence, no separate self, and inter-being is the flower. In Hanh's words in his book *No Death, No Fear:* "We can describe the flower as being full of everything. There is nothing that is not present in the flower. We see sunshine, we see the rain, we see clouds, we see the earth, and we also see time and space in the flower. A flower, like everything else, is made entirely of non-flower elements. The whole cosmos has come together in order to help the flower manifest herself. The flower is full of everything except one thing: a separate self, a separate identity."

And we might ask this piece of paper on which I write: "Piece of paper, where do you come from?" The same can be asked about the one who writes on this paper. Everything is impermanent, always changing, and transforming into something else.

With the understanding of inter-being, of our connection to everything else, without a separate existence, the enlightened person is compassionate and engages in actions to relieve the suffering of others. The awakened being helps others to become awakened and compassionate in their own suffering. The ox herder, in becoming awakened in the course of herding, takes good care of all others. In Buddhist practice, caring for others and their suffering, as you care for yourself and your own suffering, is a vow and a calling.

THE FAIR As summer ends, I have found among the books saved from the attic of the farmhouse pages from a book of my childhood, *The Three Little Pigs*. All that remains is the middle section of the book, but enough to bring back the memory of the story and its importance to me. The moral at the end of the story was, and still is, that you should build a sturdy house and be resourceful when dangers come your way.

For me, more immediate and tangible is the fact that pigs played an important part in my early life. My grandfather Will Holloway introduced me to the world of hogs. He had raised pure-bred Duroc Jersey swine on his farm north of Millard —"Wayside Oak Farm." I raised purebred Durocs until I went to college, and they helped to finance my college education. At the end of each summer, I would show them at the Walworth County Fair, and the prizes they won would ensure a good price when I sold them for breeding stock. My Durocs were raised for the perpetuation of pigs in the world.

The significance and unstated attraction of the county fair was being away from home for several days after a summer of working in the fields. During the day at the fair, I would roam the fairgrounds unattended and uninhibited. It was a time to greet neighbors on new territory. My grandfather would be in the Agriculture Building looking at the prize seed corn and the vegetables. Farmers walked around and sat on the latest improvements in machinery. Neighbors picnicked on the green and listened to the band. Others viewed horse races and special acts from the grandstand. I would stop often to listen to country music being played in the radio station tent.

In my imagination, there was something always darkly exotic about the carnival at the fair. It was a source of magic and mystery. I looked forward each year to being caught up in the sounds, vibrant colors, and crowds of the carnival. On the midway, I would see carnival men and women beckoning: a woman offering darts for popping balloons; a man with tattooed arms and an open shirt holding out three balls to knock down a stack of wooden milk bottles. Walking past a tent with an arcade of machines, I would hear loud noises and see people wandering out with cards dispensed from machines for a penny. Other sights would draw me on: motorcycles roaring inside a rickety-walled inverted dome; revolving wooden animals and dragons painted orange, teal, and red; an octopus-shaped ride ablaze with colored lights reaching up and out into the night sky.

And then there was the Ferris wheel. Up and up, around and around. Once was the summer that I finally sat at the top of the Ferris wheel with the girl of my dreams. These summers marked the end of one season and the beginning of another.

A LIFETIME BURNING How many times have I returned to the last lines of T. S. Eliot's poem "East Coker" from the *Four Quartets*? I read carefully each line and recognize the deep relevance to my own life. The world becomes stranger, the pattern more complicated, and a lifetime burns in every moment. This is the time for evening under lamplight.

> Home is where one starts from. As we grow older
> The world becomes stranger, the pattern more
> complicated
> Of dead and living. Not the intense moment
> Isolated, with no before and after,
> But a lifetime burning in every moment.
> And not the lifetime of one man only
> But of old stones that cannot be deciphered.
> There is a time for the evening under starlight,
> A time for the evening under lamplight
> (The evening with the photograph album).

A memorable season of the day, a time of awakening. We are explorers, starting from home. At once, still and still moving. Into another intensity, a deeper communion with the nature of our true being.

Rising in the eastern sky is the harvest moon, the legendary full moon that is closest to the autumnal equinox. Farmers continue to harvest their crops by the light of this the brightest of moons. We will gaze for a while at the moon as it shines in the evening sky. Here, still herding the ox, I pray the Lord my soul to keep.

Part II

World of Dreams

THE DIAMOND SUTRA I have thought about and contemplated the nature of reality for as long as I can remember. Beginning on the farm, walking the land, working in the fields, tending the farm animals, and listening to the soft words of my family as the darkness folded us into the night. And we would dream ourselves into another day.

Of late I have turned to the ancient sutra, the Diamond Sutra of the Mahayana Buddhist tradition, for an understanding of the nature of reality, of our human perception of reality. An elder monk named Subhiti asked the Buddha about reality. At the end of the Diamond Sutra is the famous four-line verse that I keep repeating to myself:

> Thus shall ye think of all this fleeting:
> A star at dawn, a bubble in a stream,
> A flash of lightning in a summer cloud,
> A flickering lamp, a phantom, and a dream.

Now, here at home, new leaves are forming on the trees surrounding my house in town. At the farm, the land is being prepared for another year of crops. The chicken house is gone, the stanchions have been removed from the barn, another farmer is herding heifers and steers, and acres of land are allotted to the growing of vegetables. And a new farm couple is living in the house my father and mother built when they were married nearly a century ago. I drive to the farm occasionally to see the beauty of the land, marsh, and wooded hills, as the seasons come and go.

I often think of Homer's hero, Odysseus, after his return to beloved Ithaca, casting an eye to another shore and yearning for fresh travel. A melancholy figure, tired and aging, but still wanting to explore. Here he is in Tennyson's poem:

> Old age hath yet his honor and his toil;
> Death closes all: but something ere the end,
> Some work of noble note, may yet be done,
> Not unbecoming men that strove with Gods.

Hardly a morning passes without my thoughts going back to the farm of my beginning. I imagine the great bur oak standing tall in the field, throughout the seasons, always a solace and a reminder that old age has its honor. Any sorrows or laments are tempered by thankfulness for this life. Songbirds are calling this morning, mating and nesting. In the course of this morning hour, I wonder what the day will bring. Might there be some work of noble note?

A WORLD OF DEW — AND YET In a Chinese sutra we are told that what is true never vanishes. What does vanish when we are mindfully aware is delusion. The Diamond Sutra proclaims that creations of the mind are like dreams, phantoms, and bubbles. Can the mind ever break out of its dream state? Let us say, at least, that being mindfully aware alters our dreams. Whether the alterations bring us closer to what is true is a question beyond our human ability to know.

If our lives are the stuff of dreams, if the mind even in awareness can never know the truth, the truth of our existence, the truth of daily reality, then what are we to do? Maybe the same as we would do if we knew the truth, could know the truth; we would live carefully and with great compassion. It could be that in not knowing we are even more careful and compassionate in the living of our everyday lives. Living without certainty of the truth makes our living more precious and meaningful. Each moment is a moment filled with the meaning that we give to our actions and to our thoughts — the meaning that we create in our daily relations with others, near and far. In not knowing, I am who I am.

Kobayashi Issa, author of the *haibun* spiritual journal *The Spring of My Life,* wrote this poem two hundred years ago:

This world of dew
Is only the world of dew —
And yet … and yet …

Yes, and *yet.* How to live with life as a dream? One goes on living carefully and with wonder. And with thankfulness.

THESE LETTERS AND THESE PHOTOGRAPHS Many letters and photographs are stored in boxes, in the drawers of chests and buffets, in attics and basements and closets of aging houses. Occasionally someone will browse a family album and try to learn more about an ancestor. How many times have I been one of these explorers of family history, hoping to know about those who lived a long time ago?

I know there is a difference between the words written in a letter and what I read now after the passing of the writer. There is a difference between the portrait of the ancestor living at the instant of the photograph and my viewing of the portrait after the ancestor has passed away. An aura surrounds the words and images of those now gone.

And there is the realization that there is a fine line, and only a fine line, between those who once lived and those of us who live today. The separation between the living and the dead vanishes readily with time. The vastness of our time of being unborn makes our living, our existing, but a drop of dew, a flash of lightning, and a dream. Unborn is our primary natural state. These letters and these photographs are reminders of our brief time among the born. Our messages remain for a while.

LIFE IN RETROSPECT Looking back on a life, you see clearly what was only glimpsed as life was being lived. Does it make any sense to lament what could have been otherwise? To think about the actions and deeds that could be changed if given the chance to relive that former time? Life — this life of dreams — is lived presently even as patterns and memories of the past and visions of the future shape it. The privilege of retrospect is possible only after the fact of living. Retrospect is a thought, a moral critique, an abstraction, rather than real life. With compassion, toward others and ourselves, we know that we are living our daily lives the best we can.

A friend recently quoted a line from the Woody Allen movie *Crimes and Misdemeanors* spoken by Professor Levy, a sage philosopher. Giving advice on how to view our lives in retrospect, he says, "We are all faced throughout our lives with agonizing decisions. Moral choices. Some are on a grand scale. Most of these choices are on lesser points. But! We define ourselves by the choices we have made. We are in fact the sum total of our choices." The sum total, I will remember that. How we have lived in the whole course of our given time is the record of our human attempt to find meaning in an otherwise unknown universe. And that meaning for us is the sense that we have done the right thing as often as possible. That our lives have been in the direction of what is good and true, good and true as far as we can know.

THE FAMILY FARM Some time ago, long after the creation of a universe and a galaxy and a planet that would

be called Earth, natives roamed this continent without claim to the land. Eventually, emigrants from other lands made the land their own. They cleared and tilled and farmed the land. They built houses, barns, granaries, and sheds for livestock and machinery.

Four generations lived on this farm in Walworth County. The farm was made of families connected by marriages and births as it slowly grew during the years. Pioneer families of the county — Holloway, Bray, Wishart, Taylor, O'Keefe, Reynolds, and Quinney.

And beyond these families were the families surrounding the farm, including Kittleson, Dutcher, Johnson, Duesterbeck, Olson, Williams, Jacobson, Keltner, Larson, Nelson, Scola, and Gies. These were the families and farms of Sugar Creek Township that you will find on the plat map of the late 1800s and the years into the middle 1900s. The many rural schools and churches that dotted the map served to make a community. It took a community to make a family farm.

Our farm of 160 acres was started as a few acres purchased in 1868 by our great-grandparents shortly after emigrating from Ireland. The farm, always a subsistence farm, survives to the present time. Our father and mother reduced the amount of farming as they aged and as their sons left the farm to seek other lives. Our mother rented the acres for thirty years after our father died. We inherited the farm with her passing in 1999 at the age of ninety-two. The farm survives intact, but it survives without the many things that once made it a family farm in a community of family farms.

The farm survives, for the time being, as land for a sustainable agriculture. We have sought to improve the land and protect the woodlands and wetlands. Still, this is a transition to what we do not yet know. The land in the beginning was not for us to own. Might the land again become a common ground? A common ground for our time here on Earth.

WE SHALL NOT CEASE FROM EXPLORATION In the Diamond Sutra, the Buddha looked within himself and found nothing fixed. Nothing separate, determinate, unchanging, no self distinguished from everything else. Only through grasping, holding on to views, do we try to halt the flow of things. Thought is itself an attempt to stop life. All beings and things are dependent on all other beings and things. We are constantly in flux, arising and dying in each moment. Change is the fundamental reality, and nothing remains the same. This fleeting world, a flickering lamp, a phantom, and a dream.

And yet I readily assume a separate self, an independence of things, and a world without change. We try heroically to preserve the family farm, trying to preserve that which ultimately cannot be preserved in the flux of time. Letting go, not being attached, would be the natural thing to do. Suffering the loss of what once existed is the price of continuing to hold on to what has no permanence. An absolute understanding is not readily apparent in this conditioned human world of ours.

These lines of poetry, from T. S. Eliot's "Little Gidding" in his *Four Quartets,* are a guide for my time of life:

> We shall not cease from exploration
> And the end of all our exploring
> Will be to arrive where we started
> And know the place for the first time.

Pressing evermore is the desire to explore the wonder that I know as my life. Exploring where I came from, remembering my years of growing up on the farm, and giving homage to the ancestors and all others who have come before me.

OUT OF IRELAND Descendants often speak the name Bridget, my great-grandmother, my father's grandmother. Bridget was born Bridget O'Keefe in 1831 in Milltown, County Kilkenny, Ireland. Scant records exist of her life. The manifests of several ships during the 1840s list her name as a passenger. Some lists have her traveling with family, and in others she is alone. You know from stories passed through the generations that she married John Quinney in 1850 while they both were living in the Irish section of Yonkers, New York. No records have been found of her life prior to leaving Ireland during the famine. She was a commoner, anonymous, not subject to the keeping of records. Maybe someone, of a future generation, and still interested, will make the journey back to Ireland and learn more about Bridget and her family history. Those who fled the famine never returned, and they talked little about their lives before leaving Ireland. I can only glimpse her life in my imagination. In the morning hour I imagine how she might speak to us in her own voice.

What would have become of us if we had stayed in Ireland? Would we have survived the famine? Would we have been sent to the poorhouse? You might wonder how we gathered the funds to pay the passage to New York. How did John and I meet, and did we know each other before leaving County Kilkenny? What was our life like in the years in Yonkers before leaving for Wisconsin in 1859?

Our daughter Kate and son Tom were born in Yonkers. Over the water and in wagons by land we made our way to the little community of Millard in Wisconsin. For several years we rented a couple of acres until we could make a down payment on the twenty acres a few miles south. This was 1868, and our family had grown with the birth of John and Bill and Mary. We lived in the house on the hill. My husband died much too young in 1880. Our

son John farmed the land and added acres to the farm.

In 1895, I traveled by train to South Dakota to visit my sons Tom and Bill and their young families on the farms they homesteaded. They had immigrated to the Dakota Territory to claim homesteads in the 1880s. During my visit we all went to the photography studio of M. B. Barton in Alexandria to have our portrait made. I posed proudly between the families of Tom and Bill. You can now look into our eyes in that photograph and image our lives. We are saying to you that we too existed.

I became an old woman, and I passed away on a February day in 1920. My daughter Kate pasted in her scrapbook the brief obituary from the local newspaper. Below the obituary she attached a poem.

I did not weep.
It seemed I did not know
'Twas endless sleep.
And time went on —
Drab days that groped or sped.
Somehow I could not learn
That she was dead.

I kept my faith to the end. Rosary in hand. I have gone to another place.

Bridget, mother of generations, you are a benchmark of my existence. In the realm of history, you are of the old world, and you came to the new world. Before you, there were ancestors from ancient times. In future historical time, there will be the descendants of us all. We of the present generation are in the midst of before and after.

Everything that has existed, and that exists now and will exist in the future, is interconnected and interdependent. In the words of the Prajnaparmita Sutra, all phenomena are marked by emptiness, neither produced nor destroyed, neither increasing nor decreasing. Nothing has a separate self, and nothing exists by itself. Everything is a part of everything else. Thich Nhat Hanh writes, "We are made of our mother and father, our grandmothers and grandfathers, our body, our feelings and our perceptions, our mental formations, the earth, the sun and innumerable non-self elements." Everything, including that which we know as ourselves, is in a constant state of creation. Understanding this, making this an integral part of our being, is to become enlightened about our true nature.

Walk by the old place where our ancestors made their home long ago. Among the lilac bushes and the remaining foundation of the old house, you will sense a presence that does not diminish with the years. You will know that you are a part of all that has ever existed. And when your heart and mind are ready, you will know that there is no birth and no death. There will be a peace, a release from the fear and anxiety of this relative

existence.

A HANDFUL OF THINGS I KNOW This morning hour I begin by imagining the life of my grandfather John Quinney, Bridget's son, my father's father. My grandfather walking across the field coming toward us as we stood by the barn is what I know to this day as my very first memory. I can only imagine how my grandfather might speak to us today.

A lifetime and beyond of being John Quinney. I was born in 1860 in a rented house near Millard shortly before Mother and Father purchased the few acres that would become the farm. I lived in the house on the hill surrounded by lilacs with an orchard that sloped to the edge of the pond. I grew up there and never strayed far from the old place. I farmed the land, and tamed and worked horses for field and plow all of my life. My two brothers, Tom and Bill, went west in the eighties to claim homesteads. Sister Kate worked much of her life in Chicago as a seamstress and milliner. Mary married Henry Reynolds and raised a family a few miles away. My dear wife, Hattie, died much too young after the birth of our three children. I never married again, and I told anyone who asked that I would never find a wife as good as Hattie. Hattie, my dear Hattie.

Our Marjorie was born in 1895, a year after we were married. Floyd and Nellie were born at the beginning of the new century. After Hattie died in 1905, I did the best I could raising the children with the help of Mother and Kate. The years went by so fast. One of my last memories is from the final year of my life, 1939, and I am walking, troubled by arthritis, across the field to the farm buildings. Floyd and his sons are watching as I slowly make my way toward them. My grandson will for the rest of his life remember this as being his first memory, and the only time he remembers ever seeing me.

There are very few living now who remember hearing anything about me. Hardly anyone remains who actually saw me. A neighbor's granddaughter recently told someone that her grandfather and I visited often and worked together with our horses. Little remains of tangible evidence that I ever existed. There is the fading photograph from Marjorie's album of me standing behind the grain drill, with the team of horses, in the field near the old house. I am standing tall with mustache, squinting into the light. This is the picture that my descendants will show of me as their ancestor. A leather harness, a feedbag, a horse collar, and a cap still hang on the dusty wall of the granary. An iron horseshoe dug up from the field has been nailed to the side of the chicken house east of the barn.

Generations later it is said that I was the best breaker and tamer of horses in the county. I do admit that I was rightly recognized as being good with horses. Many of the horses were the mustangs rounded up wild in the west, shipped to Clinton, Iowa, and bought by farmers in Iowa, Illinois, and Wisconsin. I worked hard farming the land, milking the cows, and taming the horses. I can't recall the times I did much more than work on the farm.

You could say that horses were in my blood. Blood carried in the veins of my mother and father when they came from Ireland during the famine. At night I dreamed of wild horses running in the moonlight. As I worked the fields by day, horses in harnesses made my living. You might imagine me now running and working and resting with horses.

Did I dance with another after Hattie passed away? Did I go to town on Saturday nights? Did I drink beer at the tavern in Millard? Behind my back neighbors would tell their friends, "He is a man of few words." When I talked I had a bit of the accent of the Irish, learned from my parents. But I tried hard to fit in to the ways of my emigrant neighbors from Norway, Germany, England, and Bohemia. We all knew that we were newcomers in this country, and we wanted to be accepted and not noticed as being different.

You'll find little evidence that I put pen to paper for reasons other than the occasional legal document. Two or three years before we were married, I wrote a few words with my own hand in Hattie's little red autograph book.

On February 6, 1891, I wrote in a fair, slanting script these lines to Hattie:

I Don't go much on religion
I never ain't had no Show
But I got a middlin tight grip Sir
On the handful of things I know.

I signed the autograph book as "J. Quinney, Delavan." A practical man, as you can see, with a proper wooing for a wife I had in mind even then.

Hattie and I were married in the Methodist church. Sister Kate remained a Catholic all her life. Brother Bill and his family followed the Catholic religion in South Dakota. Mary became a Methodist and passed her faith through the generations of her family. I wasn't much for church services on Sunday mornings, with my chores calling. Mother was always a Catholic of the old country. She attended Sunday morning Mass at Saint Andrew's Church, as long as she was able. In the early years she walked the five miles to the church in Delavan each Sunday morning. She had a religious faith to carry her the forty years after my father died in 1880. Father had a bit of the superstition from the old country, sometimes telling us about the little creatures that inhabited thickets, marsh, and the woodlands.

Hattie's folks were of a long line of devout Christians. Her ancestors came from England as Puritans and settled in the colonies. Her father, Nathan Church Reynolds, with the long gray beard of a prophet from the Old Testament, descended from a Salem family accused of witchcraft. His ancestors fought in the American Revolution.

The siblings of Hattie made for a large family. Her brother Seymour lived with us until the night he slipped on a patch of snow-covered ice while carrying a log back to the house to keep the fire burning throughout the cold night. We found him three days later covered in snow with his dog waiting beside him. Hattie and I kept in contact with her five sisters, who led their own tragic lives, some dying young of consumption, as did Hattie.

Hattie looks out at us with our baby in a portrait made in Delavan the year of Marjorie's birth. There is also the portrait of the six sisters, beautifully dressed, standing beside each other, with Hattie in the back row. And there is the large oval portrait of Hattie before our marriage. My son's wife wrote on the back of the portrait, for posterity, "Floyd's Mother." And there is the picture of me years later, in one of the albums, standing with neighbors in a farmyard.

Eleven years of marriage we had. Fortunate were the children and I to have had the help of Kate and Mother after Hattie left us. Throughout the years, the lamps flickered during the winter evenings in the dark rooms of the house on the hill. Kate, finally living in the house alone, survived me by a couple of years. She placed into her album the brief obituary, my death notice, from the newspaper in town.

AS LONG AS WE ARE REMEMBERED My mother kept a framed photograph of her mother, Lorena Taylor Holloway, on the table beside her chair as long as I can re- member. She died in the prime of her life, at the age of thirty-eight in 1921, of Bright's disease, when my mother was a child. The family had just moved from the farm up the road to our new house in Millard. Her husband, Will Holloway, and daughter, Alice, had to adjust to a life without wife and mother. I often think about my grandmother Lorena, and sometimes I imagine how she might speak to us about her life.

In my thirty-eight years, I lived with the stories that were told of ancestors in the few generations before me. My mother told us about her parents, James and Joyce Wishart, deceased by the time I was born. Her father had made a living as the blacksmith in LaGrange. He emigrated from England in 1828, settled for a few years in Clinton, New York, and came to Wisconsin in 1844. His father and mother, John and Ann, emigrated with him and lived the last years in LaGrange. According to the account in LaGrange Pioneers, *John was a sturdy Scot, a mason by trade, a great reader and intelligent talker, pious in character and temperate in his habits of life. Ann, with maiden name of Stockdale, is described as a woman of deep piety and noble character, and like her husband was of Scottish birth and parentage. James and Joyce had* ten children, and my mother, Ellen, always called Nellie, was the last born.

My mother married Charles Taylor, and they farmed and lived in the large Greek Revival house beside the road in LaGrange. You may have seen the photograph of our family posing on the front lawn. Little is remembered and hardly anything is told about my childhood. I know that an old newspaper clipping and a few artifacts have been found to document the tragedy of the loss of my sister, Leah, at the age of ten in 1888. In one of the family trunks was found a six-by-ten-inch black cardboard box with "Writing Desk" spelled out in embossed letters that had belonged to my sister. A few of Leah's belongings were placed in it when she died: pencilled lists of school grades, colored cards of dancing children, and a small roll of mending materials with thread, needle, and pins. There is an ornate metal plate engraved "Leah — Our Darling," and the obituary from the local newspaper.

A long time ago we children carried flowers and placed them upon the grave of my sister. My brother Leo died a year later at the age of two, and the procession again went to the cemetery on the hill. My brother Lloyd and I remained with Mother and Father to grow up on the farm.

Will Holloway, who lived on the neighboring farm, and I married on a February day in 1903. Alice, our one and only, was born in 1906. Will recorded the birth along with other notes about preparing the land for spring planting. Our family of three went about our daily chores in tune with the seasons. We visited regularly and gathered for celebrations with relatives who lived close by. Alice would become the recorder of our lives in the diary that she kept and in the many photographs she took with her camera. What you know of our family, and of me during my last years, can be gleaned from Alice's childhood diary. You can read the entries to know about our time together.

A few strands of my hair were saved in a little round box. My tattered and well-used book of hymns to save the soul survived and occasionally comes into the light of day. The hymn I pasted inside the front cover waits for another voice. I had faith that there was more to this life than what appeared. And my consolation: "When all my labors and trials are over, and I am safe on that beautiful shore." Oh, that will be glory for me.

MOTHER'S CHILDHOOD DIARY Beginning in January of 1916, when she was nine years old, my mother, Alice Marie Holloway, wrote faithfully in her diary each day for five years. I have gleaned a few entries from the diary to remind us of the life of my mother and her family when she was a young girl.

I took my camera to school. Teacher showed me how to take a picture. Teacher took a picture of me. Jack (my cat) *would not hold still so I could not take his picture. We went to Millard and back in the car. I wore my hat to school.* (May 4, 1916)

We had a short auto ride. Took Grandma's picture. I had the headache all day. Papa and I went to the woods. I took a picture of mama and papa in the car. Papa took a picture of me at night. (May 7, 1916)

Did not go to school. I was not sick. I was lazy. Papa painted some of the garage. Jack (is my cat) slept with me in the afternoon. I got up at 4:30 P.M. Papa painted the milk house. (May 8, 1916)

It was Christmas. Went up to Grandma's. Uncle Lloyd and Elsie were there. Had more presents. Got a gold thimble. (December 25, 1917)

We went to Delavan to the picnic in Tilden's woods. A soldier that had been a prisoner in Germany 2 years spoke. (August 28, 1918)

Had salt fish for dinner. (Drank water all the afternoon.) Mama and I picked ducks. Feathers all over. (October 24, 1918)

Report came that the war was over. People celebrated all day. Went to Elkhorn at night. (November 11, 1918)

Went to school. At night went to Woodmen banquet. Played games after supper. They danced. Got home about half past twelve. (February 12, 1919)

Was my birthday. Got a pair of silk gloves and silk stockings from mama and a box of candy from papa. (April 29, 1919)

Ma and pa went to Janesville after a pony. Bought Trixy. Ma drove her home. Trixy is 4 years old. (July 25, 1919)

Went to school. Grandma died in the morning. Rained. (September 30, 1919)

Cold. We did not go to church. Grandpa came down to supper. November has been cold with lots of rain. Up to now I have driven to school every day and put Trixy in Patchen's barn. (November 30, 1919)

We and Uncle Lloyd and Aunt Elsie and Grandpa went to Uncle Frank's to dinner. Snowed and drifted the night before. 18 below. We were going sleigh riding at night, but it was too cold. (January 1, 1920)

School picnic at Turtle Lake. Got my diploma and standings. Was valedictorian of my class. (June 4, 1920)

Rained. Papa went to town with oats. An aeroplane went over. (June 17, 1920)

Fine day. We all went to Racine. Aunt Rachel went with us. In the afternoon went to the shore of Lake Michigan. At night went to a vaudeville. (August 7, 1920)

Went up to Uncle Lloyd's. Mrs. Uglow and Myrtle and Elva were there. Had a swell dinner. Stayed to supper. Had oysters. (December 25, 1920)

My mother stopped writing in her diary shortly after her mother passed away. Her father lived to be eighty-six. In 1930 she married my father, Floyd Quinney. They farmed together and raised two sons. My father died tending chores in 1969, and my mother remained on the farm for the rest of her life, until she was nearly ninety-three.

A SPIRITUAL LIFE You came to consciousness and self-awareness as you watched your grandfather Quinney coming across the field from the old place. Soon after you would find yourself lying on your back in the grass in the same field, looking into the blue sky with the floating white clouds and seeing the face of a founding father of your country. You knew instantly, then, that you had been chosen, called to a meaningful life. That your life would be spiritual as much as it would be physical.

You inherited deep and steady religious traditions from generations of ancestors. Your maternal ancestors were Reformation Protestants who emigrated from the midlands of England during the first half of the nineteenth century. They carried with them the King James scriptures in well-worn family Bibles. They built Methodist churches wherever they lived as they moved westward to Wisconsin. They attended services regularly and faithfully for the rest of their lives. The cemeteries in LaGrange and Sugar Creek townships contain the remains of the ancestors that gave you body and spirit.

Your father's ancestors practiced the Catholic religion for generations before the emigration from famine Ireland. You can only speculate about the practice of religion in earlier and ancient times. Some ancestors likely carried the genetic and psychic makeup of the Celts, the Vikings, the Anglo-Saxons, and the stone-age tribes of earlier migrations across Europe. Each time you walked down to the old place—the home of the three generations that preceded you—you sensed spirits inhabiting the remains of the old house, and sensed a presence among the oaks and maples and willows. Crows in the high branches watched as you walked through the tall grass. Red-winged blackbirds sang to the coming of spring, and great blue herons flew from the tamaracks in the marsh.

The black rosaries of your great-grandmother and great-aunt rested on the dusty attic floor of the farmhouse all the years of your childhood. Each night at bedtime you said your prayer: "Now I lay me down to sleep." You prayed the Lord your soul to keep. On Sundays you learned the stories from the Bible and sang in the church choir. On Easter Sunday morning you gathered at the lake with fellow worshippers and watched once again the signs of resurrection. Not that you certainly believed the beliefs, but you knew that something, something mysterious beyond knowing, was being observed. You knew that as you aged you would always be part of the spiritual world.

The first big move of your life began as you were driven, a distance of thirty-five miles, by your parents to the college you would attend for the next four years. You were leaving the land and home of your first eighteen years of life. True, you were somewhat prepared by the years of high school in town. It had taken the freshman and sophomore years in Delavan High School to adjust to the ways and expectations of townspeople. There had been the appendectomy you insisted upon to relieve the anxiety and pains suffered each morning on the way to school. Some sense of well-being came with participation in school activities, the making of friends, and courses and classes. You learned to play the trombone, eventually fronting a dance band and playing "Star Dust" as fellow students danced in the gymnasium. All of this was well beyond the eight years in the one-room school in the country. In later years you knew that the rural school and the life of farming gave you a foundation for all that would follow.

Missed most of all during the first year of college, especially at bedtime, were the voices of your father and mother and brother. And you missed gathering around the kitchen table in the farmhouse for breakfast, dinner, and supper. You experienced the loneliness of being away from home. All the homes you have made in the course of a life have echoed the one known at the farm. Your achievements in college were a way to adapt to a world beyond the farm. Being elected president of the student body seemed to be an indication of acceptance by others. You dated and danced, and joined a fraternity to be able to live in a house at the edge of the campus. The summer between the junior and senior years you drove with a group of students from the Wesley Fellowship to a revival meeting at Lake Poinsett, South Dakota. At the end of the week, gathered around a campfire at night, you all were asked to come forward one by one to seek salvation. You were the only one who did not go forward. A spiritual life for you would have to be personal and practiced from within. Graduation from college took place in 1956 on a beautiful Sunday afternoon. Family and relatives surrounded you.

What were you to do with your life? You remember the listening and the waiting to be *called*. The question would persist throughout your life, but now was the time to make immediate decisions. You had majored in biology and psychology and sociology, and you had thought about pursuing a career in one of the medical professions. The summer spent working in the credit office of Wesley Memorial Hospital in Chicago turned you away from a possible career in hospital administration. An earlier summer of working as an orthopedic orderly in a hospital made you certain that you did not want to be a doctor. You had thoughts of being a minister, a Methodist minister like those you had known and admired while you were growing up.

Late in the summer, while working at the hospital in Chicago, you were drawn to the questions posed in your undergraduate sociology courses. You thought about the many teachers who had been important in your education. On impulse, but surely more than that, you removed your car from storage and drove up Lake Shore Drive along Lake Michigan to the campus of Northwestern University. You met with Kimball Young, the head of the Sociology Department, in his apartment in Evanston. He welcomed you to the fold, and he would be your advisor, and you would be his research and teaching assistant for the year. A grandson of Brigham Young was pointing the way for a life that could be of service to others.

For the next twenty years your spiritual life was away from theistic religion, beyond a God-centered spirituality. Graduate school presented questions that could be answered adequately in secular terms. You were told, in fact, to give up spiritual concerns in the pursuit of science. A world without God was world enough, and most likely the real one. You were well on the way to being an existentialist as well as a scientist. You would regard this as your spiritual life, one that was grounded primarily in daily life and in the family that you were now creating.

You began your university teaching career at the start of the 1960s, teaching first in upstate New York and then moving to New York University in New York City. Leaving the state of your birth and youth was important to your personal development. Your wanted to know about life outside of Wisconsin and what seemed to you at the time as the larger world. You remember asking yourself, repeatedly, as you walked the streets of New York, what is the meaning of life? The question was not new to you, just more pressing and crucial at this time. All of your life, for some reason that you do not know, the question has been on your mind in one way or another. The question has been about the meaning of your own life, but more than that, the meaning of human life in general, and beyond that, the meaning of all life on Earth, and the meaning of the whole universe. Why was the universe created, and is there any purpose to its existence? These questions have guided much of your thought and being through the course of your whole life. Coming, occasionally, as an answer of sorts, is the realization that the meaning of life is in the living of life, that living and being able to live is meaning enough. This is all the meaning that the human mind is able to know.

You became politically aware and active while living and teaching in New York. Your academic work was informed by your involvement in the civil rights and anti-war movements. You immersed yourself in the popular culture of the times. On the streets of the city, camera in hand, you intensely observed a world. You began to write each day, and your writing became part of your spiritual life, part of your calling.

As the seventies began, you decided to leave the city. Consumption, both material and cultural, began to overwhelm mind and spirit. In need of a quieter life, a more meditative life, you took a leave from university teaching and moved with your family to North Carolina for three years. There would be explorations of many kinds. You traveled and gave lectures. You wrote books. You often visited your mother on the farm, and you missed your father, who had passed away on a November day in 1969.

Providence, the city and the inspiration, would be a home for the next ten years. These would be the years of an explicit return to matters of the spirit. One day your daughter asked for participation in a religious community. This led to attendance at the First Baptist Church in America, the church founded by Roger Williams, with a minister well grounded in the neo-orthodox theology of Tillich, Niebuhr, and Bonhoeffer. Eventually you and your family would attend the services and activities of the First Unitarian Church of Providence. It was there that you began the Buddhist studies and practices that would become the basis of your spiritual life. You found what you had never lost.

A return to the Midwest, your true home, was necessary and inevitable. You were now within sixty miles of the farm, teaching sociology at Northern Illinois University. You and your family regularly visited your mother at the farm, photographed the landscape of the county, wrote daily in the journals that would become books, created friendships, and lived close to the rhythms of a deliberate life. Your younger daughter left home for college, and you became a grandfather when your older daughter gave birth. There would be a crisis and change in your household with divorce and a new marriage.

You were aging and you became ill with chronic leukemia. At the turn of the century, after you retired from teaching, you and your wife moved to Madison, finally returning to Wisconsin forty years after leaving in the summer of 1960. You found ways to preserve the family farm after your mother passed away as the new century was about to begin. There seemed to be a rounding to your life.

Others have told you that you have lived a spiritual life. From your perspective, your life has been a constant and perpetual search for meaning. You have thought of yourself as a pilgrim. Several religious traditions have been studied and integrated into your sense of who you are and how you should live. You have tried to live a good life, a life that is of service to others, a life that follows the perennial guidance of the Golden Rule of doing unto others as you would have others do unto you.

Late in your life, now, you try to maintain a faith in the wonder of existence. You seek to be fully alive in the course of aging with its pains and increasing infirmities. Engagement and optimism are part of the work of a continuing spiritual life. You greet the day with a faith in life, and you are aware that the meaning of existence is ultimately unknowable. Absolute reality will always remain a mystery. The distinction between life and death is a construct of the conditioned human mind. Your life began long before your birth. Living with the mystery of temporal existence is the essence of the spiritual life.

THE ONE WHO WRITES Returning home from visiting my daughter Anne and her family, on an autumn day a short time ago, we were three hours from home and tiring after driving all day from Memphis. Darkness was coming to the Illinois prairie. But when a sign on Interstate 55 pointed to the town of Lincoln, we exited to a road that took us along a stretch of old Route 66 for several miles on the outskirts of town. I had wanted to see, however brief the time would be, the hometown of writer William Maxwell. Decades ago I had read his book *So Long, See You Tomorrow.* Without that book, I might not be sitting at this table writing these lines about my world of dreams.

Over the years Maxwell and his biographer, Barbara Burkhardt, met to gather material about his life as a writer. In his New York apartment and at his country house north of the city, she would ask him a question and he would place a sheet of paper into his typewriter and carefully compose his answer. He could think on the typewriter better than talking, he told her. There are writers who speak eloquently in interviews. There are other writers who compose and convey their thoughts, their creations, best on paper. Is not writing, for many, the only feasible way of expressing thoughts and ideas, characters and plots and stories? In writing, only in writing, worlds are brought forth, worlds that might not exist without the imagination that comes with the writing of words. A writer's secret knowledge: I write, therefore I am.

Composing and typing his answers, Maxwell said this about his writing: "I have a melancholy feeling that all human experience goes down the drain, or to put it politely, ends in oblivion, except when somebody records some part of his own experience — which can of course be the life that goes on in his mind and imagination as well as what he had for breakfast." Autobiographical writing over the course of Maxwell's life, in a succession of books and stories, has given some degree of permanence to the lives of people he knew and loved. We, the readers, have a record of how this writer thought and what he experienced, from childhood to old age. Past and present always meet in his writing, as Maxwell's biographer notes, stretching before him like the land and sky of his midwestern landscape.

We returned to the highway, saving an extended visit to Lincoln and the sites of Maxwell's early years for another time. We turned north in the dark night and made our way home. Silently giving thanks for a visit with family now spread across this land of pioneers.

THE WRITER'S QUESTION Here in our town, in an apartment near the center of town, was born in 1897 the child who would become the writer Thornton Wilder. In the play *Our Town,* which he wrote in the mid-1930s, he has the young Emily, who has returned to Earth for one day, ask, "Do any human beings ever realize life while they live it? — every, every minute?" The Stage Manager is guiding the audience through the town of the now departed. Primal questions are being explored: How do we live? How do we survive? What is love and how does it help with the difficulties of living? And always the central question: "How do we live, knowing that we will die?"

Wilder's earlier novel, *The Bridge of San Luis Rey,* helped to support the large Wilder family of parents and often-struggling siblings. In the novel, the Abbess says in the memorable conclusion, "There is a land of the living and a land of the dead and the bridge is love, the only survival, the only meaning." But the existentialist and ever-questioning Wilder, years later in the play *The Alcestiad,* has Alcestis say, "Yes, but love is not enough. Love is not the meaning. It is one of the signs that there is a meaning." Somewhere in the living of daily life, the universal and the eternal are to be found. Later in his life, in the solitude of a desert, writing the novel *The Eighth Day,* Wilder found some consolation in the idea that we as part of nature are ever evolving. Creation has not ended.

Four days before Wilder died, his biographer tells us, he wrote friends, "I am now old, really old, and these recent set-backs have taken a lot of energy out of me." Not giving up, still with the hope of further writing, he wrote, "I think I'm pulling myself together for another piece of work."

AS WINTER COMES Jupiter appears in the night sky. And around it the constellation Orion, the Pleiades, and the bright star Hyades. A long time ago, three magi on camels crossed a desert leading to the town of Bethlehem of Judea. There had been foretelling of something miraculous about to happen. The Gospel of Matthew later would tell that the magi found mother and child and made offerings from treasure chests. The magi returned home on a path that would not take them by way of King Herod. Christian traditions would celebrate the Epiphany, the revelation that the son of God has come to earth. With a crucifixion and a resurrection, the religion of the incarnated Jesus Christ was founded.

In the poem "The Journey of the Magi," T. S. Eliot tells of the three magi making their way across the desert to witness the birth of Jesus. Told in the first person by one of the magi, they arrive in the evening—"not a moment too soon"—for the birth of the baby. "A hard time we had of it," with the thought that possibly it all was folly. Each year I listen to Eliot's recording of the poem, and I gaze at the nineteenth-century painting by James Tissot of the three magi making their way out of the mountains and into the desert. Eliot, as he writes his poem, has converted to the Anglican Church, and the old ways, for him and the magi, are fading.

He, who was born in a manger, will die on a cross. The new religion will hold the promise of resurrection and everlasting life. This time of year, centuries later, prompts a questioning of the old dispensations. Thus is life's challenge as we join the caravan crossing the desert each year as winter comes.

TRANSCENDENT DREAMS Who is this dreamer? I am recording the dreams that come to me. I am recording the life I am living. Where do these dreams come from that I bring to you? Surely, the dreams that I dream are of a much larger, collective dream. We do not dream alone.

My dreams are firmly grounded in a world of transcendence. Within my being, as they must be, but founded on all that is outside of me. I am part and parcel of the universe and perhaps a cosmos beyond the universe. I am not the first to know that I contain multitudes. That I have no separate existence, that I am everything.

And often I imagine myself as a Henry David Thoreau wintering in a cabin in the woods at Walden Pond. I am part of the long tradition of the transcendentalists. My dreaming life comes out of the philosophies of English romantic poetry, German idealism, Eastern religions, and the practical wisdom of all people seeking and living a deliberate life daily. An inner truth founded on personal intuition transcends the dreamer.

My life's calling has been that of actively observing the world. At the beginning of his account of going to live in the woods beside Walden Pond, Thoreau wrote, "For many years I was self-appointed inspector of snow storms and rain storms, and did my duty faithfully." He found a universe within himself and in the landscape close to home. He was fully employed in the daily observations and reflections that he noted in his daily writing.

This winter I think especially about Thoreau's visit to the Midwest near the end of his life. I think of him looking out the train window, far from his New England home. For years he had suffered the effects of tuberculosis. Finally in 1861, the year before he died, his doctor advised him to seek a change of climate and suggested a long journey to the West Indies or the South of France or the Mississippi Valley. Perhaps because of the lower cost of a trip to the Midwest or because of his interest in American flora and fauna, Thoreau decided to travel to Minnesota. The journey began from Concord on the eleventh of May and ended when he returned home on the tenth of July.

After stopping at Niagara Falls and Detroit for a few days, Thoreau and his traveling companion, Horace Mann Jr., a student of botany, reached Chicago on May 21. Resting for a couple of days at the Metropolitan House, and visiting a Unitarian minister, they bought tickets to Saint Paul, Minnesota. Thoreau saw the prairie for the first time as the train rolled across northern Illinois to Dunleith. From the port on the Mississippi, Thoreau and Mann went up the river by boat, stopping along the way at Prairie du Chien, Wisconsin. From their room in Saint Paul, Mann wrote a letter to his mother, saying that Mr. Thoreau "is doing very well now and I think will be a great deal better before long."

Thoreau's journal of the trip is devoted mainly to natural history. He went to geological and botanical museums, talked to naturalists, read books and reports, gathered and identified many specimens, and searched eagerly for a wild crab apple tree. He observed and noted the many species of birds and animals — wild pigeons in enormous flocks, turkey buzzards and herons, king-fishers and jays, swallows, ducks, and turtles. He showed little interest in frontier life and was embarrassed by a Sioux Indian dance staged in Redwood for the party of travelers.

At the end of June, Thoreau was ready to return home. He and Mann left Minnesota on the twenty-sixth for Prairie du Chien. They then took the train to Milwaukee, passing through Madison at one thirty in the afternoon. They reached Concord the second week of July, traveling by way of Mackinaw City, Toronto, Ogdensburg, Vermont, and New Hampshire. I think now of Thoreau, on the train, passing within a few blocks of my house.

The excursion totaled thirty-five hundred miles, the longest trip Thoreau had ever made. He had cut the trip short by a month or more, possibly because of home-sickness and certainly because of the continuing illness in his chest. Some years ago, a literary commentator, John T. Flanagan, suggested a reason for Thoreau's early return: "Possibly also he realized that there was no cure for him, and he desired to spend his final lingering days in the setting endeared to him by nature and man. In any event, he never left home again." Becoming weaker during the winter, Thoreau died on May 6, 1862.

Near the end, a friend asked Thoreau how the opposite shore appeared to him. He answered, summing up the way he had lived his whole life, "One world at a time." In a last letter, Thoreau observed the effects of the night's rain on the gravel of the railroad causeway. Thoreau concluded the letter: "All this is perfectly distinct to an observant eye, and yet could easily pass unnoticed by most. Thus each wind is self-registering." Earlier he had noted that each life is self-registering. We make our observations, take a few notes, and then we pass on.

NOTHING IS LOST You wake up in the morning after a night of dreaming. An adjustment quickly follows, bringing you into the waking state that we know as ourselves. Each morning is a new creation of our being, of who we think we are in mind and body, and name. You could not entertain your scattered state for more than a few seconds without a disturbing confusion. You put the pieces together for another day. And you wonder if you still are the person you were before the night began.

King Richard II experiences the annihilation of the self at the end of Shakespeare's play. "When time is broke and no proportion kept!" How many times, how often, do we have to put ourselves together to maintain proportion, to go on with our lives? What would it be for us to entertain brief moments of the true state of our nature? With words addressed to the Buddha, Thich Nhat Hanh writes, "I shall listen to your advice and look deeply into impermanence, interdependence, emptiness, and inter-being in order to arrive at the deep realization that all that exists has the nature of no birth and no death, no coming and no going, no being and no non-being, no permanence and no annihilation." Nothing that exists has a separate reality. Everything is interdependent and a part of everything else. At some absolute level, beyond our human calculations, nothing is lost. This is how we can think of all things, flashing across the dreams of our existence.

All things are made of other things. Nothing has a separate existence, a separate self. We are made of our parents and grandparents and all the ancestors before. We have all descended from the first humans that appeared in Africa and moved in subsequent generations to other continents. And before these people, we humans had evolved from primates, and the primates had evolved from early mammals. Our origins, human and otherwise, go back billions of years to the single cell organisms growing in moist places. And before all this, we came from the matter — never to be lost — of the universe. We have been here from the beginning.

In a comprehensive family genealogy, we all are related to each other. We are related not only to the relatives of the familial categories but also to all beings before us, and to those who will exist after our time. We are more than our family tree, related to everyone, on the tree and beyond. And ultimately we are of the matter of the cosmos. We are not alone; we are everywhere, then and now and always. Let us entertain the sweet music of the universe. Nothing is lost.

I SHOT AN ARROW INTO THE AIR Let the day begin with a valentine heart. A heart that is pierced by cupid's arrow, an arrow of love heightened with passion. This image is of classical proportions, of the gods and goddesses of ancient times. And in early Christian time, the priest Saint Valentine would die in prison with a note to the guard's daughter, signed, "Love from your Valentine."

For a long time we have sought the words and symbols to express this longing of the heart. This deep longing to be connected to others, to know the connection in our daily lives. Much depends on the heart, this vital organ of body and soul. The heart that is true, never false. With Shakespeare's first line of the sonnet: "O never say that I was false of heart."

Down at the old place, a valentine card came to me the first year of my life. Great-Aunt Kate sent cupid to pierce my heart with the arrow of love. An entry that lasted, never to heal, a love that would overcome any death. The bow was drawn and love was delivered certainly forever.

Attend this day carefully to the practice of love. The love and compassion for others and for oneself. Help others to transform their suffering into a love that recognizes our interdependence, the essence of our being.

The heart pierced by love. Thus have I heard and thus have I seen. As real a dream as ever I will know.

In the field, from planting time to harvest, you could hear my father reciting the lines from Henry Wadsworth Longfellow's poem:

> I shot an arrow into the air,
> It fell to earth I knew not where.
> For, so swiftly it flew, the sight
> Could not follow it in its flight.

You will find the poem printed in most country schoolbooks as the nineteenth century passed into the twentieth. The remaining stanzas:

> I breathed a song into the air,
> It fell to earth, I knew not where;
> For who has sight so keen and strong,
> That it can follow the flight of song?

> Long, long afterward, in an oak
> I found the arrow, still unbroke;
> And the song, from beginning to end,
> I found again in the heart of a friend.

My father, as with the poet, is telling all who will hear that those things of long ago still exist even when they are out of our sight. That which once was still is.

Such is the search for love as cupid's arrow speeds through air and time. With heart in song, the arrow goes to its destination. After many years the poet, and the one who recites the poem, knows that the arrow of love is unbroken and has landed. The arrow of love finds its perfect mark. What is sown in the springtime will reach harvest.

THE SCRAPBOOK They shared a song, my mother and father, many songs. You will see, years later, the family albums they created out of love for this family. There is no dividing line between living and dreaming. What you love and sing about and dream about are one and the same. There is no life without the dreaming. Life is the manifestation of dreams.

On the cover of the black scrapbook is a picture of a Scotsman standing on a rock and blowing a horn with his hound at his side. Inside on the first page is the clipping from the newspaper: "A son, Earl Richard, was born Wednesday, May 16, to Mr. and Mrs. Floyd Quinney at Walworth County Hospital." The year is 1934, and a card announces my arrival—"Hello Everybody!" Another card, from neighboring cousins, notes that the baby will "make home a little heaven on earth." Pages follow filled with cards from near and far of love and best wishes to the child born to this family. The design and artwork found on the pages of the scrapbook express the aesthetics of the time.

Cousin Vera in Canada sends the first Easter card to the baby. The first birthday is observed with many cards from relatives, friends, and neighbors. "Happy Birthday to a Little Man," says the card from neighbor Bernice:

> Here's a Birthday wish
> For a little lad
> For the happiest day
> He has ever had.

And another year comes with greetings for another birthday and the holidays. More cards are received, one of a boy playing an accordion that pops out of the card. The message on the card is of the power of song: "The Same Old Tune Keeps Coming Out: The Words Are 'I Love You.'"

BEARING WITNESS The things we place into the world live on long after we lose sight of them. Appearing again as artifacts found in attics and basements of old houses or, perhaps, preserved in the historical archives. These are the shards from the past. Watching yet another performance of *Hamlet*, we are reminded that there may be life beyond a void of the great unknown. Hamlet, at the death scene, tells Horatio, "The rest is silence," a silence for Hamlet. He has told Horatio to tell the story:

If thou didst ever hold me in thy heart
Absent thee from felicity awhile,
And in this harsh world draw thy breath in pain,
To tell my story.

Someday the tale of the sweet prince will be told. "Horatio, I am dead; thou livest. Report me and my cause aright to the unsatisfied." Shakespeare's play will be read and performed for centuries hence. The tales will be told another time. We are here, the living, bearing witness to the silenced lives. We are left to play the music and sing the songs.

A TELLER OF TALES "Meanwhile, I scribble on." So writes Arthur Crew Inman in his diary, a diary that began in 1919 and continued into 1963. The handwritten diary, consisting of 155 handwritten volumes, is one of the longest and most remarkable diaries ever written. The original volumes were taken from the vault of a Boston bank and edited by Daniel Aaron and published in two volumes by Harvard University in 1985.

In his darkened Boston apartment, Inman wrote an estimated seventeen million words that chronicle his life, the life of his wife, Evelyn, and the lives of at least a thousand people he knew and interviewed, as well as daily reflections — however biased — on national politics, wars and revolutions, and the social changes of the times. Inman wrote forthrightly about his fears, compulsions, fantasies, and nightmares. He rented the apartments above and below his own in Garrison Hall to shield himself from the outside noises.

The diary contains endless worries about the writer's health. According to some speculation, Inman suffered from temporal lobe epilepsy and may have had the condition known as *hypergraphia*. Anyone who has a great need to read and write daily might wonder if he or she is on the borderline of such a condition: the reading and writing daily without end, recording the dreams, giving a narrative to the dreams that dance day and night in our heads. Inman died in 1963 by a suicide that would silence the unbearable noise from the nearby construction of the Prudential Tower. It was a noise that could not be filtered out by his brain or by writing another entry in his diary.

THE TRUEST SENTENCE THAT YOU KNOW How to start your day writing? First, there must be the need; otherwise you can be doing something else, living another way. I often think of Ernest Hemingway, nearly a century ago, squeezing the peel of little oranges into the edge of the flame, waiting for the words to come. He walks to the window, looks over the roofs of Paris, and thinks to himself: "All you have to do is write one true sentence. Write the truest sentence that you know." Late in life, in his memoir, *A Moveable Feast,* he would tell us that writing stories when he was young in Paris was good and severe discipline. Writing is a way to understand your being in the world, to learn from it, and a way to go on.

In the middle of the seventeenth century, Matsuo Bashō, haiku poet of Japan, took to the open road in the spirit of Buddhist philosophy. He recorded his travels, sometimes published and titled as *Narrow Road to a Far Province.* Bashō reminds us that life itself is a journey: "Those who steer a boat across the sea, or drive a horse over the earth till they succumb to the weight of years, spend every minute of their lives traveling." This guiding idea is found throughout the Western canon, as well, in such classical works as *The Odyssey, The Pilgrim's Progress,* and *The Canterbury Tales.* For me, in various travels and writings, photographs are my poems. And I am the teller of tales. I still wake up in the morning from dreaming that I am young and ready to begin a great adventure. The awareness that comes in the morning hour is my adventure for the day.

WHEN WE WERE COWBOYS The reveries, mine being those of a cowboy, dispel any doubt that we live in a dream world. Cows grazing in the pasture on summer days, milking the cows in the barn early mornings in the winter, on my horse rounding up the cattle at the end of

the field. Throughout the summer, after chores and supper, my brother and I would listen to *The Lone Ranger.*
Riding our bicycles on the dusty road, we imagined
ourselves on the range, pursuing outlaws and rescuing
maidens. All summer I would feed and groom a Jersey
or Holstein heifer to be shown at the county fair at the
end of summer. A box of prize ribbons is stored some-
place among the treasures.

Today I listen to cowboy songs, beginning early in
the morning when the radio plays Tex Ritter's recording
of "The Old Chisholm Trail":

Come along boys and listen to my tale
I'll tell you of my troubles on the old Chisholm Trail
Come a ti yi yippy, come a tee yi yay
Ti yi yippy yi yay.

Come all you cowpunchers, come along with me on the
old Chisholm Trail.

An early version of the song by Huddie Ledbetter
(Lead Belly) was titled "When I Was a Cowboy." The
tradition of such songs began with cowboys of various origins on ranches in the Southwest. The folklorist
Alan Lomax collected songs like "Home on the Range"
and "Get Along Little Dogies" from a retired trail cook
in 1908. Many of them were a reworking of older folk
ballads that came from England, Ireland, and Scotland.

Songs soothed the cattle and kept the cowboys awake and alert through the long night.

The historical cowboy lasted only until the 1890s. But the romantic myth of the cowboy would never go away. The ballads of cowboy life — ranging from the brooding songs about death, of herding cattle and nights around the campfire, humorous songs and tales of chases and gunfights — added to the poetry and music of American culture. The cowboy myth spread around the world. Buffalo Bill Cody toured Europe with his Wild West Show, re-enacting the winning of the West and the conquest of Native Americans.

The herds of longhorn cattle had doubled in size during the Civil War and were roaming the ranges of the Southwest. Though of little value in Texas, cattle were in demand as beef in the cities of the North. This was the golden era of rounding up, herding, and driving cattle to the stockyards in Abilene, Cheyenne, and Kansas City. New railroad lines carried the cattle to Omaha and Chicago and to the cities of the East.

The first trail used for cattle drives, sometimes following the earlier Indian trails, was the Chisholm Trail. Hundreds of cowboys drove several million head of cattle over the trail. And countless versions of "The Old Chisholm Trail" were sung — in the saddle, around the campfire, and in the saloons along the way. You can still hear recordings of the song by popular singers Gene

Autry, Woody Guthrie, Roy Rogers, and Michael Martin Murphey. Classic western movies like *The Texans* and *Red River* portrayed the cattle drives over the Chisholm Trail.

Many were the tales and laments of cowboys driving cattle in all kinds of weather, across rivers and streams, into canyons and over mountains, through badlands, and fighting off rustlers and Indians. "Feet in the stirrups and seat in the saddle, I hung and rattled with them longhorn cattle." The cowboy hopes someday to quit herding cattle.

There is always a horse with a cowboy. Bareback on "Sparkplug," I was a cowboy riding into the sunset before bedtime. Grandfather Quinney made part of his living "breaking" mustangs from Wyoming into plow horses in Wisconsin. Horses were in the blood of the Irish fleeing the famine. Far from the Wild West, we rode and worked with horses as if we were cowboys. Harnesses, horse collars, bridles, and ropes hung in the barn ready for work the next morning. Today, when I walk to the garage of my house in town, I pass a bridle hanging in the doorway.

The ballad "Stewball" (sometimes called "Skewball") recalls a racehorse that triumphs because either it is faster or the other horse stumbles. Coming to America in the nineteenth century from Ireland and England, the song was sung by slaves and became widely known as a chain-gang song. Lead Belly, Woody Guthrie, Pete Seeger, and Peter, Paul, and Mary have sung versions of it. I listen closely to Joan Baez's haunting rendition from the sixties. "Stewball was a good horse. He wore his head high."

The other song that will fill the day is "Ballad of the Absent Mare" by Leonard Cohen. "Say a prayer for the cowboy, his mare's run away," sings Cohen. I have learned, to my surprise, that the ballad is based on the twelfth-century allegory of oxherding, the Zen instruction for enlightenment. Classically, the boy — the herder of the ox — searches for the ox only to discover that the ox was never missing. The ox is within the herder, the Buddha nature being in all of us. In Cohen's ballad, the mare is found, tamed, and the rider no longer needs the rein. Finally, a return to the source, equanimity, enlightenment: "And they're gone like the smoke and they're gone like this song."

The day ends with Emmylou Harris singing her version of the Leonard Cohen song — now titled "Ballad of the Runaway Horse." She sings: "Say a prayer for the cowgirl her horse ran away. She'll walk 'til she finds him her darlin' her stray."

I THOUGHT ABOUT YOU Thinking about the future and the past takes place in the present. The only real time is the present moment; all else is a construct of what might be in the future or what is imagined as having been in the past. Being mindful in the present is being attentive and alive to the moment. Mindfulness gives birth to understanding, compassion, and love. With mindfulness, we are capable of enjoying all the wonders of life.

In my solitude, these days of the week when I am home alone, while Solveig is away at work, much of my present time is of things in the past, of people and relationships, especially of family. The past is created anew in the process of writing. I am in time present as I write about things of the past.

Thinking freely in solitude moves the writer to unforeseen, unanticipated realms. Thinking in solitude is more than talk internalized, and more than the spoken word. Thinking takes place before speaking, before the shaping of thought into the verbal symbols that we know as the words of speech. A tape recording of the thoughts in your head would be quite different from a recording of your spoken words. Much is lost in talking, in speaking outside the solitude of thinking.

These thoughts in solitude are not separate from the thoughts of others. Just as we are not separate selves, not separated from others, our thoughts are a part of all thoughts that are going on at the moment. We humans are of a collective consciousness and, likely, of the consciousness of other species, and of inanimate objects as well. There is the interpenetration of everything in the world. There is no separate existence — even (and especially) in our solitude. In solitude, we experience the oneness of all. Our connection to everything that exists, has ever existed, and that will exist in the future is mindfully understood in our moments of solitude. Then we know that we are not alone.

A DEEPER VIEW OF LIFE The light in the late afternoon sky signals the coming of spring. Among the ancients, the arrival of the vernal equinox indicated that a new year was about to begin. Flowers and grasses emerged from the ground and birds began to sing. Here, this morning, little more than a week before the equinox, snow falls gently, cardinals and sparrows come to the feeder, and a squirrel gathers a few kernels from the deck.

You try to absorb the deeper view of what life is, beginning with the insight that all life is impermanent, and that impermanence is a fact that can be understood positively. Impermanence gives life its value and promotes our compassion for one another. Thich Nhat Hanh writes: "When we accept that all things are impermanent, we will not be incapacitated by suffering when things decay and die. We can remain peaceful and content in the face of continuity and change, prosperity and decline, success and failure."

The deeper view of life goes in and out of focus regularly as I live thankfully each day. Being human, we dream that we might escape the fate — the promise — of impermanence and death. Everlasting life will depend on another dream.

The Diamond Sutra ends with the observation that all composed things are like a dream. Throughout the sutra, the discourse between Subhuti and the Buddha is on being a compassionate person whose intention is to relieve our own suffering and the suffering of our fellow beings. The person on the way to enlightenment helping others, in the sutra, is called a *bodhisattva*. The bodhisattva does not have a separate identity: "Bodhisattvas will have no perception of an egoistic self, neither of a separate entity nor of a soul, no perception of a personality. Nor will they even have a perception of dharma or non-dharma, for in them there will be neither perception nor non-perception." In the heart of the bodhisattva there exists great energy called *bodhicitta*. Many people can be helped — with suffering relieved — by those who aspire to the life of the bodhisattva. All beings, we are told in the sutra, have the potential to be on the path of enlightenment and compassion. The vow is to relieve the suffering of all living beings, where peace may be realized.

Thus you have heard that all things of the mind are to be regarded as fleeting images. If you look deeply into things you will be able to be free of illusion. We live our ordinary lives knowing that all composed things are like a dream, that with compassion we can be of help to others, and that the absolute realm is one of selflessness and impermanence. Share these fruits with all beings.

PURE STATE OF SUNYATA The Sanskrit word *sunyata* is often translated into English as "emptiness." It could also be translated as "everything." Either way, the reference is to dependent origination of all phenomena. The mind creates a world of apparent separation and independence. The absolute reality is sunyata.

In the book and commentary on the Diamond Sutra from the Pythagorean Sanga, edited by Raghavan Iyer, we read the eighteenth-century verse from the seventh Dalai Lama. On being mindful of sunyata:

> All through the circle of apparent and transitory
> objects
> Spreads the space of the clear light of the real, the
> ultimate.
> In which all things have a transcendental being.
> Forsaking all mental inventions.
> Dwell in the pure state of *sunyata*.
> Draw in your mind, centering it in the real.
> Guide your attention with mindfulness.
> Holding it within the real.

Sometimes, with great care, we may dwell in the pure state of sunyata.

THE LEISURE OF AN ELDERLY PRESENT As we age, we may release ourselves from the pursuit of being immersed in the daily events of the world, locally and globally. We may come to think that it is not necessary to be up-to-date on everything that is happening in the world. That being informed and engaged is not necessarily a moral imperative at this time of life. I take heart from a decision made by the writer Doris Grumbach during her days of solitude:

> I wanted to shield myself from as much of the terrible particulars of modern existence as possible to preserve my shrinking time for, well, let me say it, pompous as it sounds, contemplation of more important questions, of generalities based on a past I have stored away for review in the leisure of an elderly present.

Many of the horrifying details of the present are held at arm's length as the wonders of solitude are being explored. And for a while, the writer notes, "without the constant presence of violence in my consciousness I knew who I was."

It is reported that when a monk asked the Buddha what is meant by the world being empty, he replied, "Insofar as it is empty of a self or anything pertaining to a self." Nothing has a separate existence, an identity of its own. Although we perceive of a world of concrete and discrete things, these things are empty of a substance and identity of their own. Beyond the conditioned mind, in the realm of the absolute, everything is part of everything else. How could we be lonely when we too are part of everything?

THE COMING OF SPRING The snow melts daily and green shoots of grass are appearing with the warming sun. Beyond the vernal equinox, days are longer than the nights. Late in the afternoon, the turkey vultures soar and circle before roosting for the night. As nature's harvesters, the vultures clean the earth of the spoils of winter. Behold, a new season is upon us.

Each spring I read Sterling North's book of springtime vignettes, *Hurry, Spring!* Written late in his life, the book is filled with remembrances of spring when he was growing up in Wisconsin. The migratory return of birds, the awakening of mammals, the flowing of rivers, the granting of one more spring. North reminds us that spring on this continent comes northward at about fifteen miles a day, starting in southern Florida in February and reaching us here in the Midwest this time of year. You could follow spring, as once did the naturalist Edward Way Teale, mile by mile, day by day.

A great gray owl, the largest of owls, has flown out of its far northern range and sits on a branch of a tall spruce tree at the western edge of town. Watchers of birds gather

daily with binoculars and cameras to record this unusual sighting. Likely this is a juvenile of its species, not yet
attached to a mate, in search of food in short supply this
spring in Canada. Eyes beam from the large gray facial
disc, an imposing presence as we watch from the street. I
will keep watch daily until this great gray owl takes flight
in pursuit of its own destiny.

THE ZEN WRITINGS OF DŌGEN I will continue my reading of the Zen writings of Dōgen, the Japanese Buddhist
teacher of the thirteenth century. This is my pursuit — a
flight often taken — of a better understanding and personal integration of dependent origination: Everything
is interconnected; everything affects everything else;
nothing exists independently of other beings and phenomena. All things and all beings are the way they are
because they are connected to all other things and beings. I am dependent on the great gray owl as it is dependent on me. Our flights and our returns are of the
same Dharma.

I study and practice Zen because enlightenment is
nothing other than the study and practice of Zen. This
Dōgen taught in the compiled writings we know as
Shōbōgenzō: Practice and enlightenment are one and the
same. We — among all things and all beings — are en-
dowed with Dharma, with the absolute reality that transcends our conditioned existence. Spiritual practice itself

is enlightenment, the realization of Dharma — absolute reality.

Absolute reality, in hermeneutical study, is sometimes the alternative concept for "God" or "the Divine." Without anthropomorphic presumption, absolute reality is the source through which all things and beings emanate. This reality is in contrast to the relative reality of a finite, humanly constructed reality. Absolute reality is the unconditional reality that transcends the conditioned mind. It is a return — in practice and enlightenment — to the source of all being. I will rest with the conclusion that absolute reality is already present and, being so, is not to be sought elsewhere in places other than daily life. Living daily is my practice and my enlightenment.

In his commentary on Dōgen, Francis H. Cook in his book *Sounds of Valley Streams* notes that one finishes reading *Shōbōgenzō* with the feeling that something of great richness, depth, and scope has been completed. He compares Dōgen's teaching and writing with the Greek tragedies, Walt Whitman's *Leaves of Grass*, Herman Melville's *Moby-Dick,* and Henry David Thoreau's *Walden.* Something very important has been conveyed, and the reader is left with a lingering sense of completion and inevitability.

Dōgen's answer to the question of what happens after we die is grounded on impermanence and the absence of a substantial self. There is no self to survive death; what happens in death is an entirely different state, not a different state of the same thing. Impermanence is not a matter of things changing, as one getting older, for instance. Cook writes: "True impermanence is grasped when we perceive that anything, material or psychic, is what it is for a brief moment, ceases to be, and is replaced by a novel state." This is the emptiness of things — the Dharma, the way things are. One's present state of being is followed by a different state. Each of us is a perfect expression of absolute reality.

Dōgen taught that fish swim in the water and birds fly in the sky. We all have our place and path in absolute reality. Our place and path must be our own ordinary life. Cook thus writes, "The way of practice and the door to truth consequently lie beneath our feet." This ordinary life, otherwise seen as mundane and ordinary, is sacred and holy. Absolute reality is in the actual living of each day. Before this day ends, I will go to the tall spruce at the edge of town and watch the great gray owl as it watches me.

WOODLANDS AND MARSHES A few miles south of town, the author Sterling North was born in 1906 on a farm on the western edge of Lake Koshkonong. I pass this widening of the Rock River as I drive to my family farm in Walworth County. North's grandparents had settled on the North farm in the 1840s. His book *The Wolfling* is based on the boyhood experiences of his father in the 1870s.

Next to the North farm was the eighty acres of the Thure Kumlien family. Thure Kumlien (1819–1888) had emigrated from Sweden after being taught by the successor to Linnaeus and graduating from Uppsala University with honors. He married a woman he had met at the university shortly after they arrived in Wisconsin. They lived in a log cabin they built on the newly purchased eighty acres of woods and wetlands. Kumlien would become a noted naturalist, teaching at nearby Albion Academy and identifying and collecting the animal and plant species of the region.

In *The Wolfling,* Sterling North's father, identified as the boy Robbie Trent, roams the woodlands and the marshes with Kumlien. With beautiful narration, North portrays what the boy learned from the naturalist. The coming of spring, for example:

> The boy knew from what he had been told by Professor Kumlien that the miracle of spring was due to the tilt of the earth, and the greater abundance of sunlight now lavished upon the Northern Hemisphere. This light and warmth first melted the snows of winter. It sent a stir of life into the seeds and roots of grass and flowers, pulled the sweet sap of the sugar maples to the very tips of the budding branches. It stimulated the

water birds and songsters into their seasonal migration northward, and told the wolves and many other animals that it was time to mate and to bring forth their young.

The boy labored for his father on the farm, and received an education in nature from his neighbor Kumlien.

NATURE EDUCATION At the farm, when I was growing up, we listened in April for the first calls of the frogs in the pond down at the old place where my ancestors made their home after emigrating from Ireland. The peeping and the croaking sounds came to us as the days grew warmer. The red-winged blackbirds returned to the pond and perched on cattails as mating territories were established. Mallards returned for nesting along the edge of the pond. Tadpoles began to swim in the shallow water, and the grasses shot up all around the pond. The red buds of the silver maples appeared early and eventually the leaves emerged. With scant time to linger and observe, spring was bringing the days that meant the beginning of work in the fields. The tilling, the planting, and the cultivating would follow as the summer progressed. The season of harvest would complete the cycle for another year.

In the world of nature at the farm, I gained much of my education and spiritual sustenance. The realization that life was becoming complex and mysterious was a gift given to me by our neighbor Burton Hanson. Sometime midway in the 1940s, Burton and his wife, Gladys, rented the house on what we called the Dutcher Place, the land and set of buildings that my father and mother had purchased a few years earlier. Next to my parents and relatives, Burton became the most important adult in my life. He was the person who brought me close to nature. Returning from one of his trips north, he brought me a section of a birch tree that had been chewed by a beaver. It is a treasure I still keep.

Burton took my brother and me fishing many evenings after a long day of work in the fields. Along Turtle Creek, we fished for bullheads and bluegills. Catching fish was incidental to walking along the banks of the creek and watching the evening come to the marsh. "Man alive!" Burton would exclaim whenever one of us caught a large fish, and when the setting sun lit up the evening sky.

Burton had skills that were in short supply as the 1940s gave way to the postwar years. He was what some called a "handyman" who could repair or build almost anything. Burton would tell me, "Anyone can make something, but a good carpenter is one who can repair his mistakes." One summer I worked with Burton, and together we built a handsome pig house on a farm several miles away.

The old farmhouse that Burton and Gladys lived in looked to the west over the woods at the edge of the marsh. Before the settlers moved into southern Wisconsin, the area had been home to Indian tribes. Arrowheads were found when my father plowed the field next to the marsh. There appeared to be burial mounds on the oak knoll. Burton would look longingly into the marsh and the woods from his house on the hill.

A few letters passed between us after I left the farm, but I eventually lost contact with Burton. I visited him once in the house he had moved to in a western suburb of Chicago after Gladys died and he had remarried. The last time I saw him was on the day of my father's funeral. Burton stood with the others for the brief time at the graveside with tears in his eyes. Afterward, in the falling snow, we both retreated to parked cars over the hill. We had not tried to speak to each other. We were now beyond the solace of words.

A SPRING SEASON Bashō, the pilgrim-poet of the seventeenth century, set out walking on a journey to the remote province of Japan's main island. On the five-month journey, he kept a record of his travel. His diary, variously translated and titled *Narrow Road to the Interior,* has become a classic of Japanese literature. I have lived a good portion of my life as a pilgrim inspired by Bashō's journey to the far province.

The spring season is making an unsteady entrance. The weekly weather forecast has been for rain and snow and sleet. Yet the sun shines through the clouds almost daily. Fog lifts in the morning and a new day, different from the one before, unfolds uncertainly. So much the better for exploring the uncharted terrain. I fill my fountain pen, wipe ink from fingers, and write a few words across the page. A journey on paper as if walking over wooded hills and through boggy marshes.

The delicate and curious chipping sparrow is tapping at the window, either for my attention or in recognition of itself in reflection. This sparrow with rufous crown will be my friend all spring and summer long. If the spiritual is being in touch with everything around and beyond us, my days with chipping sparrow will be spiritual days. In touch with one thing is to be in touch with everything. The ground of my being is known in the sight and sound of little chipping sparrow.

We watched the red fox cross the length of the yard. With spritely gait, the red fox is regarded as one of the most beautiful, yet peculiar animals walking the Earth. This fox among us has captured our imaginations and must be a resident making a home in a den in the ravine at the end of the street. He ventures through properties in search of food for mate and pups. Nocturnal by reputation, this fox is comfortable in the broad daylight of morning and afternoon. A neighbor recently saw the fox stretched out on the lawn basking in the sunshine. Our consciousness has increased with the presence of the red fox in our midst. I have placed three chicken eggs beneath the maple as invitation and sustenance for the passing fox.

Each graceful step of the fox brings me to the awareness of the sacredness of each present moment. There is peace and happiness and well-being as I give attention to the here and now. I see myself in connection to the generations — ancestors and those to come — and to everything on Earth. My home territory, with red fox, is in every breath and step. With mindful watching, we recognize our true home.

Good news comes today of the birth of my first granddaughter. She will be named Aurelia. She joins the generations that make our human chain on this planet. And this morning I am dancing with the daffodils. Springing from the nooks and crannies of the yard are the golden heads truly marking the season. From my window above the yard, I am in reverie with William Wordsworth.

> For oft, when on my couch I lie
> In vacant or in pensive mood,
> They flash upon the inward eye
> Which is the bliss of solitude,
> And then my heart with pleasure fills,
> And dances with the daffodils.

The daffodils dance as I return to the making of a few words to the day.

DREAMING AND WRITING In the evenings, I am reading slowly, once again, the eloquent writing of novelist James Salter. His new novel, written late in life, has an epigraph of Salter's own making:

> There comes a time when you
> realize that everything is a dream,
> and only those things preserved in writing
> have any possibility of being real.

The protagonist of the novel is giving close attention to the course of his life, and to the memories of that life that remain in the telling.

This ordinary and everyday life that we remember is also the construction of a new dream. It is the memory — the composing of a memory — that is the new reality. With the Diamond Sutra before me daily, I know that memory — the writing of the memory — is also a dream. The work of the mind in reverie and reflection is no less compelling for being a dream. The dream is now the reality, as relative as that reality may be.

A robin swoops low over the garden. Migrating white-throated sparrows are feeding in the newly grown grass below. A large blue jay dashes among the branches

of the locust tree. No doubts now about the certain arrival of spring with noontimes warmed by the sun.

FAMILY RESEARCH I find more information about my
aunt Marjorie, my father's sister whom I never met. In
the census for 1930, she is living in the household of a
family in Evanston, Illinois. Her relation to the head of
the house, William Williams, is listed as that of "Serv-
ant." She would have been thirty-five then.

The great experiment known as Prohibition ended
in 1931. That year Marjorie became part owner of a business, purchasing with a friend the Shingle Inn located on
Highway 14 a few miles south of Delavan. They ran the
tavern, which had been a bootlegging operation during
Prohibition, until Marjorie died unexpectedly in 1935
of a ruptured appendix. In probate court, bank funds
amounted to $581.06, plus $35 in cash and a 1930 Ford
coupe. Other material items of value consisted of liquor,
tobacco and cigarettes, candy and nuts, glassware, two
tables and six chairs, a radio, cash register, and a cabin
with three beds.

Before the brief time of being part owner of the
Shingle Inn, Marjorie had worked as a maid in houses around Delavan Lake, and for a while as a maid in
the Wisconsin School for the Deaf in town. While other
women of her age taught in country schools and married
farmers, Marjorie took another direction. She has been,

for me all my life, a woman of mystery and inspiration. In a photograph from her album, Marjorie stands at the old place, dressed in fine clothes, and looks toward the farm in the distance. For many years I have kept a framed portrait of Marjorie on my desk.

By the looks of things, this will be a rain-filled day. Wet, and gray, and I am happy enough. In the background, Waylon Jennings is singing "My Heroes Have Always Been Cowboys." Great resonance for me midway in the song this day: "Cowboys are special with their own brand of misery from being alone too long." This is neither a complaint nor a lament as a gentle rain keeps falling.

TRAVELING WITH FRESH EYES Bashō, in his *Knapsack Notebook*, translated by Sam Hamill, expounds on the art of the travel journal. He tells us that it is easy to observe the mundane — overcast skies in the morning becoming sunny in the afternoon. He writes, "Nothing's worth noting that is not seen with fresh eyes." Bashō's random observations and experiences along the way — in a secluded house in the mountains or in a lonely inn — linger in the mind and heart of the reader. Our observations can touch and stir the heart and mind of the reader. Bashō observes this about his writing:

> I write in my notebook with the intention of stimulating good conversation, hoping that it will also be of use to some fellow traveler. But perhaps my notes are mere

drunken chatter, the incoherent babbling of a dreamer. If so, read them as such.

With Bashō, we are in good company as we travel and make our notes about what we have seen and what we have thought.

A poet of similar sensibility, Lucien Stryk, a friend of mine, passed away earlier this year. He was a practitioner and noted translator of Zen poetry. He wrote poems of everyday life, focusing on simple and familiar details. Born in Poland in 1924, he soon moved to Chicago with his family. He studied at several universities, served in World War II, taught for years at Northern Illinois University, and was a poet all his life. I was fortunate to be a colleague of his, and to be given kind and generous encouragement by him in my own writing. In our town amid the cornfields, Lucien was the sage and the poet.

Included in his book of poems, *And Still Birds Sing*, published in 1998, is his translation of a modern Japanese haiku poem (by Santoka) — simple, elegant, mundane, and transcendental:

To the end of time,
journeying,
cutting toe-nails.

Our human journey to the end of time; our personal journey in the course of a lifetime. Life truly is a journey as we attend daily to the requirements of body and soul. What more could there be?

AN ABSOLUTE REALITY Horse-drawn buggies on Sunday afternoon were on the road as Solveig and I neared the small town of Kingston. We passed the well-kept farms of Amish families. Calling my brother later, I was informed that the Amish do not have church buildings. Services are held at various households. A large white wagon carries chairs and pews from house to house. The wagon is parked at the front of the house for a week or more, and then pulled to the next house where services will be held during the week. Services last most of the day, led by local members, and there are programs for children and there is Bible study. Meals are prepared and served. Most of the church funds are to help members in times of need.

The day of travel passed as all things pass in this dream world of ours. At night, before turning off the bedside light, I read a meditation on impermanence prepared by Thich Nhat Hanh:

Touching impermanence deeply, we touch the world beyond permanence and impermanence. We touch the ground of being, and see that what we have called "being" and "nonbeing" are just notions. Nothing is ever lost. Nothing is ever gained.

A day of being reminded that even the impermanence that we experience is an illusion. There is a reality beyond our notions of permanence and impermanence, an absolute reality.

FARTHER DOWN THE LINE I have received a package in the mail from my poet friend Mark Vinz containing his latest book of poems. When needing to read a poem about living in this midland that we share, I turn regularly to one of the poems in his book *Long Distance*. The poem "Directions" has a middle stanza on the sense of place in traveling.

> My father couldn't understand the
> trouble I had with directions. Every time
> I'm lost I think of him, the country sense
> I never had—the way he always knew
> just where we were, the quickest routes,
> the name of every crop in those mysterious
> fields, and where to find the best cafés.

Mark and I each have an ever-expanding file of our correspondence over many years. Letters about our families, our travels, the weather, our writing, and of the inspiration and help we are giving each other. About ten years ago I traveled to his university in Minnesota to give a lecture on writing about and photographing the

Midwest. With other writers from the English department, we spent an evening in a hotel bar and restaurant across the Red River in Fargo. We often remind each other of that evening, and last year in a letter I told Mark of the lyrics in Lyle Lovett's song "Farther Down the Line."

> So let's have a hand for that young cowboy
> And wish him better luck next time
> And hope we see him up in Fargo
> Or somewhere farther down the line.

Mark wrote back saying he had recently attended a magnificent Lovett concert in a new open-air theater just south of Moorhead. Just down the line from Fargo.

WHEN WORDS COME On a day in the middle of May in 1689, Bashō began his journey on the narrow road to the interior. With brush in hand, he writes these words in his journal: "A few old friends had gathered in the night and followed along far enough to see me off from the boat. Getting off at Senju, I felt three thousand miles rushing through my heart, the whole world only a dream. I saw it through farewell tears." He then composes the first haiku of the journey.

> Spring passes,
> and the birds cry out — tears
> in the eyes of fishes.

He begins his journey with the sorrow of departure. "Those who remain behind watch the shadow of a traveler's back disappear."

The words that I now write across the page, where do they come from, and why? There is much speculation on the origin of the words that make a language for us. We could just as well add the idea that words fostered the evolution of our ability to walk upright. Much depends upon words, and on the placing of words in a sequence to form sentences. And with a few sentences, the writer constructs the unit we call a paragraph. Then paragraphs into sections, and at some point a book may be completed. Or the manuscript is placed in a drawer or closet, and perhaps forgotten forever.

What was important at the beginning was the need and desire to begin the writing of words. Writing words on a tablet, a wall, or on paper when speaking was not enough. Possibly the intent was to leave a message, a message that we were here. Words to signal that that we, indeed, once existed. And sometimes there might be a story to tell. A story that is as much myth as it is historical or current event. A story that tells us what it is to be human and living this life. The writing of a story is the composing of a dream.

A beautiful sight this morning as sunlight streams across the writing table. The purple orchid is silhouetted in the window. Jay, cardinal, and the newly arrived catbird are perched on the feeder as the squirrel jumps from tree to the balcony. I listen to "The Lark Ascending" by Ralph Vaughn Williams. The *New York Times* waits to be read sometime during the day. I have posted on the wall a quote by Emerson: "I cannot remember the books I've read any more than the meals I have eaten; even so, they have made me." The garden below has been prepared for planting. Nothing more needs to be done today.

DEPENDENT ORIGINATION The Dalai Lama will be giving a public lecture — titled "In Praise of Dependent Origination"— to an audience of thousands. There will be sessions on consciousness and brain research at the university, and monks will be meditating at the Deer Park Buddhist Center. A Tibetan prayer wheel filled with millions of mantras is being installed at the Center. Each rotation will provide purification and spread blessings to the world.

To live one's everyday life naturally and spontaneously, with love and compassion, is the path of Zen. Although sounding simple and obvious, living with the naturalness of our original nature is difficult, and requires training and concentrated attention. The process is noted in a famous Zen saying:

Before you study Zen, mountains are mountains and rivers are rivers; while you are studying Zen, mountains are no longer mountains and rivers are no longer rivers; but once you have had enlightenment mountains are once again mountains and rivers again rivers.

Enlightenment consists of becoming what we already are from the beginning. As with the famous Zen metaphor, it's like riding an ox in search of an ox.

Beyond the constructions of thought, we may see things clearly, naturally as they are. Eventually realized is the interdependence of all things, the selfless existence of everything. Mountains and rivers, and everything else, are dependent on all things in their origination. With enlightened mind and eyes, mountains and rivers are seen directly, beyond the blinders of thought and discourse.

Zen practice is about returning to the ground of our natural being, realizing what we were born with and what is already waiting to be realized in the course of a life. We live in the present, relative reality, but know that in absolute reality everything originates dependently. A few years ago, in the course of my life, on a sunny afternoon, I watched the Dalai Lama approach as the crowd gathered at Deer Park.

RIGHT PERCEPTION Shunryu Suzuki would tell of mountains and rivers, about perceiving them before and after studying Zen. We are reminded by John Cage in one of his indeterminacy stories, with music, that once Suzuki was asked, "What is the difference between before and after?" He responded, "No difference, only the feet are a little bit off the ground." When the absolute realm has been glimpsed, and remembered, one lives with greater spontaneity and naturalness. Clothes are less heavy and one's step is lighter to the ground. Right perception is my hope. All is in bloom — lilac, crab apple, sand cherry, and dogwood. An offering placed early in the morning on the lawn awaits red fox. I know that every day is a new beginning.

THE PATHLESS WAY Many times, when walking together or visiting each other in our homes, Bruce and I would ask each other "What do you know for sure?" Trained as a biologist, Bruce von Zellen brought together the seemingly disparate teachings of science and the spiritual wisdom of Buddhism. He came to Buddhism the way most of us in the West come to it: out of need. How are we to bring some balance to our restless, inquisitive minds, especially ones trained to achieve and to excel?

The course was set in our explorations. Bruce would continue to remind us, following Krishnamurti, that the way is a pathless way. Stay close to the moment; our only reality is in the here and now. Take good care of the moment, and all will be well. But then Bruce would add, "There are no *shoulds* and no *oughts*." We recited the lines of the *Dhammapada* often: "All that we are is a result of what we have thought."

Bruce and I often discussed the latest finding or spec- ulation from astrophysics, cosmology, cellular biology, or medical research. Bruce would expound with great delight on a report in the morning's *New York Times*. On other days, he would say firmly, "Richard, it's just thought." We read together Seung Sahn's book *Only Don't Know*. The phrase "only don't know" became one of our understandings together. And it was always good for a laugh.

We would read and talk about the writings of Alan Watts and the poetry of the Taoists. We read aloud the Zen poetry of Ryōkan:

My hut lies in the middle of a dense forest;
Every year the green ivy grows longer.
No news of the affairs of men,
Only the occasional song of a woodcutter.
The sun shines and I mend my robe;
When the moon comes out I read Buddhist poems.
I have nothing to report, my friends.
If you want to find the meaning, stop chasing after so
    many things.

I have heard it said that we live as long as we are remembered. Bruce passed away several years ago. I delivered the eulogy at his memorial service knowing that any celebration was just another way to mourn. I noted that I would rather be at other places on that day: driving west with Bruce over the Illinois prairie on our way to the Trappist monastery in Iowa. We would be listening to a tape of Jack Teagarden playing Duke Ellington's "Sophisticated Lady," or Stan Getz on tenor sax on "I Can't Get Started," "Stella by Starlight," and "I Thought about You." On a Saturday evening, our families might be together by candlelight around the dinner table. From the beginning of our time together, I knew that I was witnessing an extraordinary life, one cloaked in the ordinariness of the everyday life.

COMPOSING A HYMN A road trip yesterday down to Elkhorn to visit the staff at the Walworth County Historical Society and to look again at some of the family albums that we deposited in the archives after clearing out the farmhouse several years ago. I was given a tour of the newly acquired building that is being called the Heritage Center. And I walked again through the rooms of the Webster House.

Joseph P. Webster wrote the hymn "Sweet By and By" in this house in 1865, with the lyrics by S. Fillmore Bennett. The well-known refrain:

In the sweet by and by,
We shall meet on that beautiful shore.

In the sweet by and by,

We shall meet on that beautiful shore.

There is a description of the writing of the hymn in the scrapbook of clippings saved by my great-aunt Kate. We are told that the hymn was written, words and music, in less than an hour and was inspired by a temporary fit of depression that overtook Webster. It is related that Webster went into the home of his friend Dr. Sanford F. Bennett in a despondent mood. The doctor asked what was the trouble. "It is no matter, it will be all right by and by," was Webster's reply. This remark acted as a flash of inspiration to the two of them. Bennett immediately sat down and wrote out the verses, and Webster composed the music on his violin. Less than an hour later they were singing the hymn with two friends.

Joseph Webster continued to teach music in Elkhorn, and wrote the song "Lorena," which became famous after the Civil War. My mother's mother was named Lorena, along with many other girls of the time. Late in the afternoon, after my visit to the Webster House, I made certain to pass the farmhouse where Lorena was born. The refrain of "Sweet By and By" still echoing in my head and heart.

PRECIOUS TIME TOGETHER A ring of the bell, and in the doorway appears a Jehovah's Witness. And we will have our midweek conversation, sitting comfortably in the living room, finding scripture to justify whatever the subject. This time our attention turns to cosmology, and the question of whether anything can come from nothing. Apparently the Bible says it's so; I think that was what we found.

I have not had such conversations since the passing of my good friend and colleague Al Meyer. Born in Denmark, he was well versed in the existentialism of Kierkegaard, and his research as a physicist took him into the realm of quantum physics. We talked together for years, and he and his wife, Cele, gave us comfort when I was ill and being treated for the blood disease. At the memorial service for Al, a few years later, I repeated some of the stories Al and I told each other as we waited by the railroad track for the train carrying atomic waste through town. Al had cautioned all his life against nuclear power, his protest grounded in the research he had done early in his career at Oak Ridge. At the service, I said that sometimes Al and I would greet each other: "How are things going?" with the other responding, "Things could be worse." I must have been trying to make the point that now I was feeling that things could not be worse.

We had talked by the tracks that day as we protested the transport of nuclear waste across the Illinois prairie. I have imagined that day as the two of us being

like the vagrants in Samuel Beckett's *Waiting for Godot*.
I remember the lone tree beside the train station. At
the service, I noted another image: Pancho and Lefty
in Townes van Zandt's song as sung by Willie Nelson
and Merle Haggard. "Living on the road my friend," and
later in the song, "He only did what he had to do." The
loaded train passed by and we demonstrators returned
to our homes.

We had wondered, Al and I, what if the quantum
physics of the subatomic world reached into our world?
Al would tell the story of Schrödinger's Cat, the cat that
had no separate existence until it appeared in an experiment. Something about the probability that nuclear decay will release the mechanism that holds the poison that
will destroy the cat, the cat being both dead and alive at
the same time. The Boy in Beckett's play asks, "What am
I to tell Mr. Godot?" The vagrant Vladimir answers, "Tell
him you saw us." That we exist, waiting to be seen.

We are clueless, I had to add, at the edge of the
abyss, not really knowing what is happening. I repeated
my mantra from the Diamond Sutra: "All things are like
a dream." Life as we know it is a fantasy, an illusion, a
shadow with no substance of its own. All things are like
dewdrops, and life is like a flash of lightning. Even so, we
share precious time together. We talked about the meaning of life, about the mystery of our existence. We were
fortunate, alive and happy.

ONCE UPON A SUMMERTIME Other seasons have come and gone and now we are slipping slowly into another summer. Garden soils are still too wet for planting, but all around foliage is green and lush and growing through the rainy days. How many summer beginnings do you recall? You may remember clearly only a few, maybe only three or four. This one I will remember because of the attention that I am giving to this Zen daybook of mine. And this summer is all the sweeter being informed by a sense of a precious few.

This summer begins with the voice of June Christy singing "Once Upon a Summertime." Listen to this song by Johnny Mercer and Michel Legrand, recorded by Christy at the beginning of the summer of 1977, and you will remember how this summer began. Each summer begins only once. What happens during that summer happens only once. Fortunate we are to be here, at this time, at the beginning of summer. Each summer happens once in a lifetime.

THANK YOU A weekend of searching in the cabinet drawers filled with cards and letters accumulated over decades. In the drawers are the cards from friends traveling, the notes written inside art cards, the holiday cards sent throughout the seasons, the notices for memorial services, the greetings from former students, the birthday cards and wishes from family and friends, the valentine cards of love, and the many cards from my daughters as they have made their lives after leaving home. There are inclusions of poems and photographs. And among the buried treasures are the cards sending a thank-you.

Thanking one another is the glue, the expression of love that holds our lives together. A thank-you conveys appreciation for a deed or gift, or simply an appreciation for being. The last written note from my mother was in a thank you card that expressed all our time together: "Thank you for all the things you have done for me." This card of thanks I place on top of a bundle of cards tied with a ribbon.

These cards will be evidence of lives and relationships. Who we were and how we lived will be known by other generations as long as these cards—these artifacts—remain. A long ago past, a past receding further each year, will be more knowable for those who will pass this way. Shards from our lives, cards saved and not otherwise lost. As in a midsummer night's dream, spirits dance, fairies fall from the sky, creatures come out of the woods and dash across the lawn, and fireflies flash in the evening.

The tomato plants, after the night of soft rain, are growing in the garden below my window. A large flicker, vividly patterned, hops over the lawn feasting in the anthills. A dove walks along the rail of the balcony. Mid-morning sunlight falls to earth through the branches of the flowering locust tree. A chipmunk darts among the rocks at the edge of the garden.

ALL THE SUMMERS OF MY LIFE The summers when I was young have shaped all the summers of my life. It is like the first sounds of creation echoing though the billions of years of the expanding universe. I am aging one year at a time, with new experiences each year, but the passing years are imprinted with the first experiences of youth. My summers, even with my aging — especially with my aging — carry the sounds and elements of long ago.

I still have the thoughts and sensations from summers a long time ago. The crops have been planted in the fields; the green tips of corn have emerged from the warming soil; and the fields of alfalfa, clover, and timothy are maturing for a first cutting. Hay will be loaded onto the wagons, pulled to the barn, and unloaded into the mow.

Following the haying season will come the long days of cutting and binding the grain. My brother and I will hitch the Oliver tractor to the grain binder, and all day long we will go over the oat field adjusting the levers of the cutting blade and releasing the bundles. I am wearing a dust mask, outfitted with a penlight battery, to alleviate my hay fever caused by the dusty grain. I likely will be complaining to my father that I am being worked too hard. As I drive the tractor over rough and hilly fields, I have visions of kids in town playing and loafing while I am working all day in the hot sun.

At the end of the summer, the threshing machine, owned and worked cooperatively with several farm neighbors, will be pulled to the field and placed south of the barn. One of my favorite photographs, taken by my mother with the Kodak box camera, shows the threshing machine, powered by the old tractor turning the long and twisted belt, blowing straw into the air and into the growing stack. One man is on the horse-drawn wagon, pitching grain bundles into the hopper of the thresher; another stands atop the enormous machine, tending the threshed oats. A white leghorn hen is in the lower left-hand corner of the photograph, a photograph that captured one fleeting moment in this fleeting world, a photograph that will hold my imagination, my dreams, over a lifetime.

THE ACT OF MEMORY I have been reading the correspondence between Eudora Welty and William Maxwell, over the course of their adult lives, in the book *What There Is to Say We Have Said,* a gift from my daughter Anne. Both of us are longtime readers of these two writers. The letters have led me this morning to read the last page of Welty's book *One Writer's Beginning* on the place of memory in our lives. "The memory is a living thing — it too is in transit. But during its moment, all that is remembered joins and lives — the old and the young, the past and the present, the living and the dead." Welty notes that her life has been a sheltered life, yet "a sheltered life can be a daring life as well. For all serious daring starts from within."

Time not capable of being reversed, we move back through it in memory. In our memoirs, in our writings during the morning hours, we return to the times remembered of love and living, and loss, and what we know of being human in our particular time and place. It is with memory, with time recalled, that we realize our humanity. Memory, the entertaining of our thoughts of the past, is part of our search for our true nature. Enlightenment is experienced in the act of memory, in the living present of the here and now.

THE MAILBOX I once made a simple drawing of one of the most familiar sights that I remember from growing up on the farm. How many times in those years did I look out the living room window of the farmhouse, directly west across the fields, to the farm of my cousin Gail? All the seasons of the year, and all the times of the day, I knew that my cousin was nearby. Her grandmother Lizzie and my grandfather Will were sister and brother.

The mailbox, standing to this day, was a reminder that even out in the country we were connected to a larger world. So much depended on the mailbox and the coming of the mailman. A walk across the yard to the mailbox was travel that lasted throughout the lives of my father and mother, and was what I knew of travel when young. Do we not still wait for the delivery that will take us, however briefly, to another place? We savor the moments of transport — and of return. My time at the table writing in the morning is like a trip to the mailbox to find what the day might bring.

HERDER OF DREAMS Time has passed since I began writing and telling these tales. Did the blade of the diamond cut through the illusions, through the constructions of reality that appear to us as dreams? Our spiritual enlightenment is the awareness of this dream world. This awareness is itself enlightenment. We are the masters, the herders, of our dreams.

Autobiographical writing is a surrendering to one's life. In the attention that we give to our days, writing is an attempt to create a self in the face of an ultimate reality where there is no self that is separate from everything else. The true self interpenetrates and is indistinguishable from all other energy and matter in the universe. This realization transcends any anxiety we might experience in daily life. We write — in the morning hour — to attend to the existential loneliness of being human. In the writing, we recognize our mortality, our transience, and the precariousness of our hold on this existence. We write in the morning hour to approach what we might know as enlightenment.

THIS STAGE ON WHICH WE MOVE AND HAVE OUR BEING
We have inhabited a dream world and, as Prospero declares in Shakespeare's *The Tempest*, "Our revels now are ended." We throw the book of tales into the sea. In this relative reality of a dream world, we know the impermanence of our existence and the mortality of our lives. Prospero imagines that our lives are dreams that fade into nothing.

> We are such stuff
> As dreams are made on, and our little life
> Is rounded with a sleep.

All of this is true in the relative world of dreams. But we remember the fruit of this quest: imagining a realm beyond our dreams. In the meantime, we are the herders of our dreams, tellers of the tales we share with others, and keepers of the wonders of our existence here on earth. We give thanks for this stage on which we move and have our being.

Afterword

The awakening hour — the most memorable season of the day — can transpire any time of day. Thoreau tells us that this quality of the day, this "expectation of the dawn," is the highest of the arts. Much of the day might be a perpetual morning.

In giving attention to our lives, to what we experience in daily life, we offer a mirror by which others can see their own lives. The personal life of each of us is of universal importance and consequence. We all are of this common stream of human evolution and consciousness. We all attempt to find meaning in our daily existence. This journal to which I attend in some way each day helps me to be mindful in the course of daily life.

The Buddha, in the Diamond Sutra, tried to help Subhuti unlearn preconceived notions of reality. Instructing us all that human thought cannot completely grasp reality. We see through a glass darkly as we attempt to perceive what is happening. We know that thoughts, both concrete and abstract, are mental constructs that mask the true reality.

For us, humans in the transience of our lives, the Buddha offers "the middle way." We are to give our attention to daily meditation and to living a life of compassion. It is enlightenment enough to be meditating and to be practicing right action. This is the life of a pilgrim on a spiritual journey.

Knowing ultimate reality is beyond our human capacity. But what is left is our responsibility to create and apply constructs of thought that make us compassionate and lead us to acts of kindness. We are active participants in the thoughts we think and in the lives we lead in relation to these thoughts. We are constantly borrowing the constructions all around us. Our thoughts are filled with literary references, with the creative constructions of others. We choose to use the constructions that come to us in the course of our search for enlightenment.

The true nature of reality can never be known to us, certainly not in our current state of evolution as a species. But through our meditation and our practice — our morning hours — we can be aware of our conditioned existence, of the human condition. And realizing our conditioned existence, and the transience and the impermanence of this existence, we live our lives with care for ourselves and for one another. We recognize that we do not have a fixed identity, a separate self, but that we are a part of everything. This is world enough.

List of Sections

Part I **Ox Herding**

Mindfulness in the Morning Hour 13
Travels at Home 13
Evening Prayer 14
Ox Herding 16
Love Among the Ruins 19
The Natural World 21
The Earth Will Remember Us 22
A Train in the Night 23
The Unborn 26
Telling the Story 28
Call of the Sirens 30
The Marsh 32
School Days 33
The Eternal Now 35
Journey to a Far Place 36
All Is Divine Harmony 38
A Shooting Star 40
Our Ancestors 41
A Metta Blessing 42
Tonglen Practice 44
And Then What? 45
The Pasture at the Farm 46
The Diary of 1939 48
Crossing the Street 50
The Blacksmith 52
Equanimity 54
A Great Adventure 55
Once Upon an Island 57
Not to Be Forgotten 61
In This World 63
A Postcard 66
Prepare a Ship 68

Swallowtail Butterflies 69
Inter-Being 70
The Fair 71
A Lifetime Burning 73

Part II World of Dreams

The Diamond Sutra 77
A World of Dew—And Yet 78
These Letters and These Photographs 80
Life in Retrospect 81
The Family Farm 82
We Shall Not Cease from Exploration 83
Out of Ireland 84
A Handful of Things I Know 88
As Long As We Are Remembered 93
Mother's Childhood Diary 95
A Spiritual Life 98
The One Who Writes 106
The Writer's Question 108
As Winter Comes 109
Transcendent Dreams 110
Nothing Is Lost 114
I Shot an Arrow into the Air 116
The Scrapbook 118
Bearing Witness 119
A Teller of Tales 120
The Truest Sentence That You Know 121
When We Were Cowboys 122
I Thought About You 126
A Deeper View of Life 128
Pure State of Sunyata 130
The Leisure of an Elderly Present 131
The Coming of Spring 132
The Zen Writings of Dōgen 133
Woodlands and Marshes 135
Nature Education 137
A Spring Season 139
Dreaming and Writing 142
Family Research 143
Traveling with Fresh Eyes 144
An Absolute Reality 146

Farther Down the Line 147
When Words Come 148
Dependent Origination 150
Right Perception 151
The Pathless Way 152
Composing a Hymn 154
Precious Time Together 155
Once Upon a Summertime 158
Thank You 158
All the Summers of My Life 160
The Act of Memory 161
The Mailbox 162
Herder of Dreams 163
This Stage on Which We Move
    and Have Our Being 164

Bibliography

Adyashanti. *Falling into Grace*. Boulder, CO: Sounds True, 2011.

Auden, W. H. *For the Time Being*. New York: Random House, 1944.

Bashō, Matsuo. *A Haiku Journey: Bashō's Narrow Road to a Far Province*. Tr. Dorothy Britton. New York: Kodansha International, 2002.

——. *Narrow Road to the Interior and Other Writings*. Ed. Sam Hamill. Boston: Shambhala, 2000.

Burkhardt, Barbara. *William Maxwell: A Literary Life*. Urbana: University of Illinois Press, 2005.

Cage, John. *Silence: Lectures and Writings*. Middletown, CT: Wesleyan University Press, 1961.

Calhoun, Charles C. *Longfellow: A Rediscovered Life*. Boston: Beacon Press, 2004.

Chah, Achaan. *A Still Forest Pool*. Ed. Jack Kornfield and Paul Breiter. Wheaton, IL: Quest Books, 2004.

Cook, Francis H. *Sounds of Valley Streams: Enlightenment in Dōgen's Zen*. Albany: State University of New York Press, 1989.

de Maistre, Xavier. *A Journey Around My Room* and *A Nocturnal Expedition Around My Room*. Trans. Andrew Brown. London: Hesperus Classics, 2004.

The Diamond Sutra. Santa Barbara, CA: Concord Grove Press, 1983.

Eliot, T. S. *The Complete Poems and Plays of T. S. Eliot*. London: Faber and Faber, 1969.

Fitzgerald, F Scott. *The Great Gatsby*. New York: Scribner's 1996.

Flanagan, John T. "Thoreau in Minnesota." *Minnesota History* 16 (March 1935): 35–46.

Flesch, William. *British Poetry: 19th Century*. New York: Facts on File, 2010.

Grumbach, Doris. *Fifty Days of Solitude*. Boston: Beacon Press, 1994.

Hamill, Sam, and J. P. Seaton, eds. *The Poetry of Zen*. Boston: Shambhala, 2004.

Hanh, Thich Nhat. *The Diamond That Cuts Through Illusion: Commentaries on the Prajnaparamita Diamond Sutra*. Berkeley, CA: Parallax Press, 2010.

——. *The Heart of Understanding: Commentaries on the Prajnaparamita Heart Sutra.* Berkeley, CA: Parallax Press. 2009.

——. *No Death, No Fear: Comforting Wisdom for Life.* New York: Riverhead Books, 2002.

——. *Touching the Earth: 46 Guided Meditations for Mindfulness Practice.* Berkeley, CA: Parallax Press, 2008.

Hardwick, Elizabeth. *Sleepless Nights.* New York: Random House, 1979.

Hemingway, Ernest. *A Moveable Feast.* New York: Scribner's, 1964.

Hill, Robert W., ed. *Tennyson's Poetry.* New York: W. W. Norton, 1999.

Homer. *The Odyssey.* Trans. Robert Fagles. New York: Viking Penguin, 1996.

Inman, Arthur Crew. *The Inman Diary: A Public and Private Confession.* Ed. Daniel Aaron. Vols. 1–2. Cambridge, MA: Harvard University Press, 1985.

Irmscher, Christoph. *Longfellow Redux.* Urbana: University of Illinois Press, 2006.

Iyer, Raghavan, ed. *The Diamond Sutra with Supplemental Texts.* Santa Barbara, CA: Concord Grove Press, 1983.

Kornfield, Jack, ed. *The Buddha Is Still Teaching: Contemporary Buddhist Wisdom.* Boston: Shambhala, 2010.

Kwong, Jakusho. *No Beginning, No End: The Intimate Heart of Zen.* Boston: Shambhala, 2010.

LaGrange Pioneers. Walworth County, WI: LaGrange Ladies' Aid Society, 1935.

Lawrence, D. H. *Complete Poems.* New York: Penguin Books, 1993.

——. *Last Poems.* Ed. Richard Aldington and Giuseppe Orioli. New York: Viking Press, 1933.

Loori, John Daido. *Two Arrows Meeting Mid-Air: The Zen Koan.* Boston: Charles E. Tuttle, 1994.

Maezumi, Hakuyu Taizan. *The Way of Everyday Life.* Los Angeles: Zen Center of Los Angeles, 1978.

Marrs, Suzanne, ed. *What There Is to Say We Have Said: The Correspondence of Eudora Welty and William Maxwell.* Boston: Houghton Mifflin Harcourt, 2011.

Merton, Thomas. *New Seeds of Contemplation.* Boston: Shambhala, 2003.

Muir, John. *A Thousand-Mile Walk to the Gulf.* Ed. William Frederic Badè. Boston: Houghton Mifflin, 1998.

Nāgārjuna, and Kaysang Gyatso. *The Precious Garland and the Song of the Four Mindfulnesses.* Trans. and ed. Jeffrey Hopkins, Lati Rimpoche, and Anne Klein. London: G. Allen and Unwin, 1975.

Niven, Penelope. *Thornton Wilder: A Life.* New York: HarperCollins, 2012.

North, Sterling. *Hurry, Spring!* New York: E. P. Dutton, 1966.

——. *The Wolfling: A Documentary Novel of the Eighteen-Seventies.* New York: E. P. Dutton, 1969.

Peattie, Donald Culross. *The Natural History of North American Trees.* Boston: Houghton Mifflin, 2007.

Quinney, Laura. *William Blake on Self and Soul.* Cambridge, MA: Harvard University Press, 2009.

Red Pine. *The Diamond Sutra: The Perfection of Wisdom.* Berkeley, CA: Counterpoint, 2001.

Ricks, Christopher. *Tennyson.* New York: Macmillan, 1972.

Ryōkan, *One Robe, One Bowl: The Zen Poetry of Ryōkan.* Trans. and intro. John Stevens. New York: Weatherhill, 1977.

Salter, James. *All That Is.* New York: Alfred A. Knopf, 2013.

Salzberg, Sharon. *Lovingkindness: The Revolutionary Art of Happiness.* Boston: Shambhala, 1995.

Shakespeare, William. *The Riverside Shakespeare.* Ed. G. Blakemore Evans and J. J. M. Tobin. 2nd ed. Boston: Houghton and Mifflin, 1996.

Shields, David. *Enough About You: Adventures in Autobiography.* New York: Simon & Schuster, 2002.

Sogyal Rinpoche. *The Tibetan Book of Living and Dying.* New York: HarperSanFrancisco, 1992.

Stewart, Harold, trans. with essay. *A Chime of Windbells: A Year of Japanese Haiku in English Verse.* Rutland,VT: Charles E. Tuttle, 1969.

——. *A Net of Fireflies: Japanese Haiku and Haiku Paintings.* Rutland, VT: Charles E. Tuttle, 1960.

Stryk, Lucien. *And Still Birds Sing: New and Selected Poems.* Athens, OH: Swallow Press, 1998.

Stury, Cecile Houghton. *The Blacksmith's Daughter.* Dallas, TX: Triangle Publishing, 1961.

Suzuki, Shunryu. *Zen Mind, Beginner's Mind.* New York: Weatherhill, 1982.

Teale, Edwin Way. *North with the Spring.* New York: Dodd, Mead, 1951.

Tennyson, Charles. *Alfred Tennyson.* New York: Macmillan, 1949.

Thoreau, Henry David. *Walden.* Ed. J. Lyndon Shanley. Princeton, NJ: Princeton University Press, 1973.

Vinz, Mark. *Long Distance.* Fairwater, WI: MWPH Books, 2005.

Wada, Stephanie. *The Oxherder: A Zen Parable Illustrated.* New York: George Braziller, 2002.

Waddell, Norman, trans. with introduction. *The Life and Teaching of Zen Master Bankei.* San Francisco: North Point Press, 1984.

Welty, Eudora. *One Writer's Beginnings.* Cambridge, MA: Harvard University Press, 1984.

——. *The Optimist's Daughter.* New York: Random House, 1972.

Worster, Donald. *A Passion for Nature: The Life of John Muir.* New York: Oxford University Press, 2008.

Worthen, John. *D. H. Lawrence: The Life of an Outsider.* New York: Counterpoint. 2005.

A Note About the Author

In a series of books, Richard Quinney has documented the course of a life that combines the everyday world of experience with the transcendent dimension of human existence. Chronologically, these works include *Journey to a Far Place, For the Time Being, Where Yet the Sweet Birds Sing, Once Again the Wonder,* and *A Lifetime Burning.* His years of photographing, with similar meditative attention, are illustrated in his books *Things Once Seen, Once upon an Island, A Sense Sublime,* and *Diary of a Camera.* He is the founder of the independent press Borderland Books. His life and work are grounded in the generations of family farming in Wisconsin. He has had a career as a professor of sociology in American universities.